veggie comfort food

veggie comfort food

Josephine Ashby

Contents

Salads   115

Cakes, Treats and Desserts   153

Introduction

The recipes in this book are based on the idea
that food is one of the great pleasures of life
and, at its finest, can be a feast for all the senses.
This book is proof that vegetarian meals can
be appealing to the eye, delicious to the taste
buds and comforting to the body.

Veggie Comfort Food takes much of its inspiration from the edible plant kingdom with its rich array of colours, flavours, tastes and textures. The key ingredients are vegetables, pulses, grains, nuts, seeds and oils. Dairy products, eggs and honey are used in some recipes but most can be adapted for those who don't eat these foods.

This collection of comfort-filled recipes has evolved over the past 25 years of experimenting with combining foods in creative ways. Over that time, the recipes have been tried, tested and devoured by large and small groups, families, friends and children of all ages. On the whole, the recipes are fairly simple to put together so home cooks, as well as those catering for large groups, will find plenty of ideas whatever the mood, appetite or occasion.

While many people may not wish to become fully vegetarian, there is a growing awareness of the benefits of reducing meat consumption – not only to human health but also to that of the planet. The recipes in this book can be enjoyed by vegetarians, vegans and meat-eaters alike. Many of them are also gluten-free and dairy-free so there are plenty of options for those with food intolerances or preferences.

The recipes are flexible and adaptable so feel free to substitute the ingredients suggested with those that are available locally, or with seasonal alternatives. With reduced food miles and increased freshness, seasonal food is both better for the environment and for us. Farmers' markets, box schemes, farm shops and local greengrocers make seasonal, locally grown fruit and vegetables widely available.

While planning meals a week in advance may suit some people, for others this is unrealistic, and for those people in particular, one of the keys to eating delicious home-cooked meals every day is to keep a well-stocked kitchen. As well as a good range of fresh fruit and vegetables, there are some basics it's worth having in the store cupboard. These include dried and canned pulses, a selection of whole grains and a range of nuts and seeds. Ingredients for enhancing the deliciousness of your meals include olive oil, toasted sesame oil, tamari soy sauce, mustard, creamed coconut, lemons, tahini, herbs, spices and cider vinegar. For those who eat animal products, eggs, cheese, yogurt and butter are also handy.

A final note regarding kitchen equipment. Most of the recipes can be made without the need for fancy kitchen gadgets. However, a food processor can be a blessing for the time-pressed cook. If a food processor feels like too big an investment, a hand blender is invaluable for making blended soups and dips. Apart from that, a decent knife will save many a cut finger, a good peeler can be a joy, and a wooden chopping board is a friend for life. Then away you go!

The following symbols are used in the recipes
For those marked * follow the recommendation on choice of ingredients

DF	EF	GF	SF	V	WF
Dairy-free	Egg-free	Gluten-free	Sugar-free	Vegan	Wheat-free

Small Plates

Whether it's lunch at home or work, a late
supper or Sunday brunch, these small plates
are designed to be versatile and easy to put
together. The wraps, dips, patties, pancakes and
fillings can all be mixed and matched according
to taste. They work well in combination with
each other to create a buffet or tapas-style meal in
which diners can assemble their own tailor-made
platters. Weather permitting, many can also be
packed up and taken on a picnic.

Buckwheat Pancakes with Guacamole

The batter for these buckwheat pancakes can be made in advance and stored, covered, in the fridge for up to a day. It is good for making small pancakes but if you want to make larger ones, you'll need to add a little more water or milk to create a thinner batter. Guacamole makes a good filling for savoury pancakes. To make sweet pancakes, add 1 teaspoon of ground cinnamon to the flour, and serve the pancakes with jam and cream, or lemon juice and maple syrup.

DF* GF

Serves 4

110g/4oz buckwheat flour
½ tsp salt
1 free-range egg, beaten
240g/8½oz natural soya yogurt
  (or other natural yogurt)
240ml/8fl oz water
butter, olive oil or coconut oil,
  for frying

For the guacamole
2 ripe avocados, peeled and stoned
juice of 2 limes
2 ripe plum tomatoes, finely diced
sea salt and freshly ground
  black pepper

DF
use soya yogurt and olive or coconut oil

Combine the flour and salt in a mixing bowl and make a well in the centre.

Combine the egg, yogurt and water in a jug, then gradually beat the mixture into the flour until you have a smooth batter. Leave to rest for an hour or more.

Meanwhile, make the guacamole. Mash the avocado flesh in a bowl. Add the lime juice and mix well, seasoning with salt and pepper to taste. Cover until ready to serve.

Heat a little butter or oil in a frying pan and drop tablespoons of the batter into the pan. Cook for a few minutes until the undersides are starting to brown before gently turning them over and cooking the other side for a couple of minutes until browned. Remove the pancakes from the pan to a warm place and continue frying until you have used all the batter.

Pile the guacamole on the pancakes and top with the tomatoes – or roll up larger pancakes – to serve.

Creamy Almond Butter and Lettuce Wraps

The crunchiness of romaine and little gem lettuce leaves makes them ideal as wraps. However, pitta breads, tortillas and taco shells also make good vehicles for this creamy, crunchy filling. Almond butter is available from health stores and some supermarkets, but if you can't find it, you can use other nut butters or tahini instead.

DF GF V

Serves 4

8 tbsp almond butter
4 tsp tamari soy sauce
juice of 2 lemons
about 200ml/7fl oz water
4–5 carrots, grated
150g/5oz alfalfa sprouts
150g/5oz mung bean sprouts
2 romaine or 4 little gem lettuces,
  separated into leaves
sea salt and freshly ground
  black pepper

Mix the almond butter with the tamari and most of the lemon juice until all the ingredients are combined, then gradually blend in just enough water to create a creamy consistency.

Combine the grated carrots, alfalfa sprouts and mung bean sprouts in a bowl. Sprinkle with the remaining lemon juice and season with salt and pepper.

Spread each lettuce leaf with almond butter and top with the carrot and sprout mixture. Eat immediately!

Savoury Seed Truffles

These savoury truffles are quick to make and require no cooking. They are perfect for packed lunches or picnics and can be stored in the fridge for a few days in an airtight container. Grated carrot can be added to the mix for extra flavour. Serve with a green salad and oat cakes for a healthy lunch.

DF GF V

Serves 4

50g/2oz pumpkin seeds
50g/2oz sunflower seeds
2 tbsp tahini
a pinch of cayenne pepper
juice of ½ lemon
a handful of coriander
a few drops of water (optional)
sea salt and freshly ground
    black pepper

Put the seeds in a food processor and grind thoroughly.

Add the tahini, cayenne, lemon juice and coriander and season with salt and pepper. Process until the mixture holds together, gradually adding a few drops of water if necessary to help the mixture bind together.

Shape the mixture into walnut-sized balls.

Avocado and White Bean Mash Tacos

Corn tacos can be bought from most supermarkets. They provide a crunchy shell that contrasts with the creaminess of the bean mash. Other white beans, such as butter beans or haricot beans, can be used instead of the cannellini if you prefer. The mash should have some texture so don't aim to make it completely smooth.

DF GF V

Serves 4

2 ripe avocados, peeled and stoned
2 x 400g/14oz cans cannellini beans, drained
juice of 1 lemon
a few basil leaves
2 tbsp olive oil
8 taco shells
a little chopped red chilli
1 lime, cut into wedges
sea salt and freshly ground black pepper

Put the avocado into a bowl, roughly chop it and then mash it.

Add the cannellini beans and lemon juice and mash them all together, leaving a bit of texture in the mash.

Tear up the basil leaves and add to the mixture. Stir in the olive oil and season with salt and pepper.

Place the taco shells on a baking sheet and bake in the oven on 180°C/gas mark 4 for 4–5 minutes until crispy.

Remove the taco shells from the oven and fill them with the mash, putting any remaining filling in a bowl. Sprinkle with the chilli and serve immediately with lime wedges to squeeze over the top.

Tartines

A tartine is an open sandwich, usually toasted. They are quick and easy to make and very versatile. You can use any type of bread but it's worth getting something tasty. Here are a few options but feel free to experiment. Each of these recipes serves one but the ingredients can be increased to serve any number of people.

Ricotta and Rocket Tartine

Each tartine serves 1   DF*

2 slices of seeded bread
2 tbsp ricotta cheese
a handful of rocket
  leaves
sea salt and freshly
  ground black pepper

Toast the bread, then spread the ricotta on the top.

Top with the rocket leaves and season with salt and pepper to taste.

DF
|
use nut or seed
butter instead
of ricotta

Tahini, Tomato and Watercress Tartine

DF V WF

2 slices of rye bread
2 tbsp tahini
1 tomato, sliced
a handful of watercress leaves
sea salt and freshly ground black pepper

Toast the rye bread and spread on the tahini.

Top with the sliced tomato and watercress leaves and season with salt and pepper to taste.

Grilled Tomato and Pesto Tartine

2 slices of crusty bread
2 tbsp pesto
1 beef tomato, sliced
a drizzle of olive oil
sea salt and freshly ground
  black pepper

DF V

use vegan
pesto

Toast the bread and spread on the pesto to cover the slices completely.

Place the sliced tomato on top. Drizzle the tomato with olive oil and sprinkle with salt and pepper to taste.

Place the tartines under a hot grill for a few minutes to gently toast the tomato slices until they soften and bubble. Serve at once.

Soft-boiled Eggs with Asparagus Soldiers

The British asparagus season lasts only a couple of months, beginning in early May, and that's the time to treat yourself to this wonderful vegetable. If you store your eggs in the fridge, remember to take them out an hour or more before making this to help prevent the shells from cracking when you lower them into the hot water.

DF*

Serves 4

4 large eggs, at room temperature
20 asparagus spears
4–6 slices of bread
4 tsp butter or olive oil
sea salt and freshly ground
   black pepper

Bring a small pan of water to the boil. Sit an egg in a slotted spoon and dip it in and out of the water a couple of times before lowering it into the water, then repeat with the remaining eggs. The dipping helps prevent the shells from cracking. Simmer for 5 minutes.

Meanwhile, steam the asparagus spears for a few minutes until just al dente.

Toast the bread.

Once the 5 minutes are up, remove the eggs from the boiling water and place them in egg cups.

Spread the toast with butter or olive oil, slice into thin strips (soldiers!) and place on serving plates. Lift the asparagus out of the steamer and arrange on the plates.

Once at the table, slice the tops off the eggs. Put a small amount of butter or olive oil into each egg, grind on some salt and pepper to taste, and dip the asparagus and toast soldiers into your eggs.

DF

use olive oil

Pea and Basil Purée with Chinese Leaves

Frozen peas are a must-have stand-by ingredient, being quick to cook, healthy and versatile. This pea purée is easy to make as well as being delicious and loved by both children and adults. As an alternative to the Chinese leaves, serve it on toast, with jacket potatoes, in a tortilla wrap or as a dip. The pea purée can be made in advance and stored in a covered container in the fridge for a couple of days.

DF GF V

Serves 4

4 tsp olive oil
2 garlic cloves, finely chopped
600g/1lb 5oz frozen peas
about 250ml/9fl oz water, plus
   extra to thin the purée
a bunch of basil leaves
1 head of Chinese leaves, separated out
salt and freshly ground black pepper

Heat the oil in a large saucepan and sauté the garlic for 1–2 minutes.

Add the peas with enough hot water almost to cover and heat for a few minutes until the peas are cooked, stirring occasionally.

Add 2 tablespoons cold water and the basil leaves, then blend everything to a purée with a hand blender or in a liquidiser. Add enough of the remaining water to create a thick purée consistency.

Transfer the purée to a bowl and sprinkle with salt and pepper. Serve the Chinese leaves filled with the pea purée.

Pan-fried Green Beans with Almonds

This recipe effectively steams the beans in the liquid provided by the lemon juice, tamari and water. As no water is drained away, all the nutrients and flavours are retained. The oil also helps to seal in the nutrients and the flavour. It can be served with rice or couscous, so put these on to cook first so they are ready at the same time as the beans. It can also be served cool as a salad, in which case stir in some chopped tomatoes and rocket leaves for extra colour, texture and flavour.

DF GF V

Serves 4

2 tbsp olive oil
1 tsp finely chopped root ginger
1 garlic clove, finely chopped
450g/1lb green beans, such as
  runner beans, French beans
  or sugar snap peas, sliced into
  2cm/¾in lengths
grated zest and juice of ½ lemon
a dash of toasted sesame oil
1 tbsp tamari soy sauce
2–4 tbsp water
2 tbsp blanched almonds
sea salt and freshly ground
  black pepper

Heat the oil in a pan, add the ginger and cook for a few minutes. Add the garlic and cook for a minute, stirring occasionally.

Add the sliced beans, lemon juice, toasted sesame oil, tamari and 2 tablespoons of water. Cover the pan with a lid and cook for 5–10 minutes until the beans are just cooked, shaking the pan occasionally and adding more water after a couple of minutes if they start to dry out.

Meanwhile, toast the almonds in a dry pan over a medium heat for about 4 minutes, shaking the pan occasionally, until the almonds are lightly browned. Tip them out of the pan to prevent them from over-browning.

Stir the almonds and lemon zest into the beans, season with salt and pepper to taste and serve immediately.

Roasted Root Vegetables with Gado-gado Sauce

This is an autumn-winter version of roasted vegetables – you'll find crown prince squash mainly in farmers' markets but butternut squash is readily available in supermarkets. A summer version can be made with courgettes, peppers, aubergines and broccoli. Leaving the peel on the winter squash saves time and effort and stops the squash from falling apart in the roasting process. It's also nutritious, providing both fibre and nutrients. However, those who don't like it can easily remove it once it's cooked. Another tip is to toast the squash seeds in the oven with a sprinkling of salt or tamari – they make a delicious crunchy snack and are packed with nutrients.

DF GF V

Serves 4

For the vegetables
450g/1lb winter squash, such
   as butternut or crown prince,
   deseeded and cut into large chunks
1 swede, peeled and cut into
   large chunks
4 beetroots, peeled and cut
   into quarters
4 parsnips, peeled and cut into
   chunky batons
4 carrots, cut into chunky batons,
   or left whole if small
2 sweet potatoes, peeled and cut
   into large chunks
4 tbsp olive oil
sea salt
a few small sprigs of rosemary
   and thyme

For the sauce
2 tbsp olive oil
2 tsp finely chopped root ginger
1 garlic clove, finely chopped
a pinch of cayenne pepper
4 tbsp smooth peanut butter
juice of 1 lemon
2 tbsp tamari soy sauce
about 450ml/¾ pint water

Preheat the oven to 220°C/gas mark 7.

Spread the vegetables out in a single layer onto baking trays. Drizzle with the olive oil and sprinkle with a little salt. Toss gently to coat in the oil. Scatter the rosemary and thyme sprigs on top.

Roast the vegetables for 50 minutes, giving them a stir haltway through. If you are not using a fan oven, swap the trays that are on the lower shelf with the ones on the top shelf at the same time.

Meanwhile make the gado-gado sauce. Heat the oil in a pan, add the ginger and cook for a couple of minutes.

Add the garlic and cayenne and cook for another minute.

Turn down the heat and add the peanut butter, lemon juice, tamari, and 120ml/4fl oz water. Stir well to incorporate the water into the peanut butter. Add more water gradually and continue stirring until you have a smooth, pourable sauce.

Once the vegetables are cooked, serve them drizzled with the gado-gado sauce.

Japanese Noodle Bowl

Rice noodles make a nice change from wheat-based pasta and cook in just a couple of minutes, making them perfect for a quick meal. For extra protein, add some diced tofu or mung-bean sprouts. Any vegetables can be used in this noodle bowl. Good options include mushrooms, asparagus and purple-sprouting broccoli.

DF GF V

Serves 4

2 tbsp olive oil
1 tsp toasted sesame oil
1 tsp finely sliced root ginger
2 spring onions, finely sliced
2 carrots, cut into thin strips
750ml/1¼ pint boiling water
400g/14oz rice or buckwheat noodles
1 tbsp tamari soy sauce
1 tbsp rice wine (optional)
110g/4oz frozen edamame beans
50g/2oz frozen peas
a handful of coriander,
   finely chopped
sea salt

Heat the olive and sesame oils in a wok or large saucepan. Stir in the ginger, spring onions and carrots and cook for a few minutes.

Pour in the boiling water and bring it back to the boil, stirring. Add the noodles, tamari, rice wine, if using, edamame beans and peas. Return to the boil and cook until the vegetables and noodles are just tender – about 5 minutes for rice noodles and 8 minutes for buckwheat noodles.

Season with salt and serve garnished with coriander.

Cheesy Corn Cakes with Rocket and Tomato Salad

These are quick and easy to make as well as being delicious! They can be made in advance and gently reheated on a baking tray in a warm oven. They also work well served cold so are perfect for picnics and lunch boxes.

GF

Serves 4 as a starter or side dish or 2 as a main course

50g/2oz cornflour
½ tsp salt
¼ tsp baking powder
2 large eggs
110g/4oz Red Leicester cheese, grated
260g/9¼ oz can sweetcorn, drained, or frozen sweetcorn
a little milk or water
olive oil or butter, for frying
2 handfuls of rocket or salad leaves
2 plum tomatoes, chopped
1 tbsp olive oil
½ tbsp lemon juice
sea salt and freshly ground black pepper

In a large bowl, combine the cornflour, salt, baking powder and eggs.

Stir in the grated cheese and sweetcorn. The aim is to get a thick batter. If the mixture seems too wet, add more cornflour. If it's too dry, add milk or water.

Heat a little oil or butter in a heavy-based frying pan until it starts to sizzle. Drop in spoonfuls of the corn mixture and flatten them slightly with the back of a spoon. Cook for a couple of minutes until crispy and golden on the underside.

Turn them over and cook for a couple of minutes until golden on the other side. Remove the cooked corn cakes from the pan and keep them warm while you continue cooking the rest of the mixture.

Combine the rocket and tomatoes in a bowl, season with salt and pepper and drizzle with olive oil and lemon juice. Serve with the corn cakes.

Cheesy Polenta

In this dish, the polenta is allowed to cool and set, after which it can be served as it is or griddled. If you are using quick-cook polenta, you will need less water, so check the instructions on the packet. It can be made in advance and kept, covered, in the fridge until it is needed. You can use any cheese but mature Cheddar, Parmesan or Red Leicester all work well. For a vegan version, use sundried tomatoes or olives instead of the cheese. Serve with a green salad for a light lunch or as an alternative to potatoes, rice or pasta as part of a main meal. Being transportable, it makes a good alternative to sandwiches in a lunch box or for a picnic.

DF* EF GF

Serves 4

about 1 litre/1¾ pints water
(check the instructions on the
polenta packet)
1 tsp salt
150g/5oz polenta
50g/2oz cheese, grated
2 tbsp butter or olive oil, plus
extra for greasing

To serve
a green salad

DF

use sundried
tomatoes instead
of the cheese

Put the water and salt into a large pan and bring to the boil. Once it is boiling, slowly pour in the polenta, stirring all the time to avoid clumps forming.

Cook the polenta according to the instructions on the packet. This could be anything from as little as 3 minutes for quick-cooking polenta to 45 minutes for slow-cooking polenta. Stir frequently to prevent sticking.

Once the polenta is cooked, turn off the heat and stir in the cheese and butter or oil.

Grease a 20cm/8in square dish or line with baking parchment. Spread the polenta mixture in the pan and level the top. Leave to cool, then cover and refrigerate.

Remove from the fridge an hour before serving. Slice into squares and serve cold with a green salad, or griddled on a hot griddle pan.

Chestnut and Almond Cutlets

With their soft texture and sweet, nutty flavour, chestnuts increase the comfort factor in any meal! These cutlets are perfect for a vegetarian Christmas dinner or special occasion. Serve as a starter, side dish or main meal with roasted vegetables and lashings of gravy.

DF GF V

Serves 4 as a starter or 2 as a main course

225g/8oz vacuum-packed chestnuts
50g/2oz ground almonds
1 tbsp tamari soy sauce
1 garlic clove, finely chopped
1 tbsp chopped coriander or parsley
1 tsp ground cumin
1 tbsp olive oil

To serve
roasted or steamed vegetables
  and gravy

Preheat the oven to 180°C/gas mark 4 and line a baking tray with baking parchment.

Put the chestnuts into a food processor and blend briefly. Add the ground almonds, tamari, garlic, herbs and cumin. Blend again. If the mixture is a bit dry, add a dash of water.

Shape into small balls and flatten into rounds about 2cm/¾in thick. Brush the cutlets with olive oil and place them on the prepared baking tray.

Cook in the oven for 20–25 minutes, turning them once halfway through, until browned on both sides. Alternatively, fry the cutlets in olive oil or butter for about 15 minutes until browned on both sides.

Serve with roasted or steamed vegetables and gravy.

Sweet Potato Patties with Tahini Sauce

These can be served with my Tahini Sauce (opposite) as a light lunch. They can also be served as an accompaniment to an omelette or a bean salad. Adding an egg to the mixture helps to bind the potatoes but it's not absolutely necessary so it is not included here.

DF GF V

Serves 4

900g/2lb sweet potatoes, peeled
   and cut into chunks
8 tbsp buckwheat flour or rice flour
6 tbsp chopped coriander or parsley
olive oil, for brushing
sea salt and freshly ground
   black pepper

To serve
1 quantity Tahini Sauce
   (opposite)

Steam the sweet potatoes for about 10 minutes until soft, then transfer to a bowl and leave to cool slightly.

Preheat the oven to 190°C/gas mark 5 and line a large baking sheet with baking parchment.

Mash the potatoes lightly, then work in the flour, salt, pepper and chopped herbs. It's often easiest to use your hands. Gradually add a little more flour, if you need it, until the mixture is thick and holds together. With lightly floured hands, shape the mixture into golf-ball-sized balls, then flatten these into patties about 2cm/¾in thick.

Brush the patties with olive oil and place on the prepared baking sheet. Bake in the oven for 20–30 minutes until browned.

Alternatively, heat a little oil in a frying pan over a medium heat and fry the patties for 5–10 minutes on each side until golden brown.

Serve with Tahini Sauce.

Tahini Sauce

Tahini is a great store-cupboard staple. Made from sesame seeds ground into a paste, it can be spread on toast, used as a sandwich filling or stirred into porridge or grains at the end of cooking to give a nutty flavour. Making it into a sauce increases its versatility further. It's a perfect accompaniment to cooked vegetables, salads, falafels, cutlets and patties. It's also one of the richest plant sources of calcium, making it a good option for those who don't eat dairy products.

DF GF V

Serves 4

110g/4oz tahini
juice of 1 lemon
4 tsp tamari soy sauce
a little water
2 tbsp finely chopped parsley,
  coriander or chives

Cream together the tahini and lemon juice. Mix in the tamari and enough water to create a thick sauce.

Stir in the chopped herbs.

Mushroom and Olive Melts

Large, flat mushrooms are perfect vessels for filling with whatever toppings you fancy. The cheese and garlic used here make a classic filling, but caramelised onions with a sprinkling of breadcrumbs also works well.

GF*

Serves 4 as a starter or side dish or 2 as a main course

6 large flat portobello mushrooms, stalks removed
2 tbsp olive oil
1 garlic clove, finely chopped (optional)
85g/3oz feta cheese, cut into small cubes
2 tbsp finely chopped parsley
freshly ground black pepper
6 pitted black olives
85g/3oz Gorgonzola cheese, cut into 6 slices
1 tbsp chopped parsley

To serve
buttered toast and grilled tomatoes

Brush the mushrooms all over with half the olive oil and grill them for 4–5 minutes on each side until softened.

Mash together the garlic, feta, parsley, black pepper and the remaining olive oil in a bowl. Fill the cavity of each mushroom with the feta mixture.

Place an olive in the middle of each mushroom and top with a slice of Gorgonzola.

Place under a hot grill and grill for about 15 minutes until the cheese is bubbling.

Sprinkle with the parsley and serve on slices of hot buttered toast with grilled tomatoes.

GF

use gluten-free bread

Sweet Potato Bubble and Squeak

This is a twist on traditional bubble and squeak, which is usually a mash-up of leftover cooked potatoes and cabbage. The sweet potatoes add vibrancy and a honey-like sweetness but it is, of course, fine to use ordinary potatoes. The Brussels sprouts add texture but, again, you could substitute them with cabbage or kale.

DF* GF V

Serves 4

450g/1lb Brussels sprouts, halved
4 large sweet potatoes, cut into chunks
4 tbsp olive oil or butter
4 garlic cloves, finely chopped
½ tsp freshly grated nutmeg
4 tbsp hazelnuts, toasted (see page 24)
sea salt and freshly ground black pepper

To serve
vegetarian sausages or soured cream

DF
use olive oil and serve with chutney

Steam the Brussels sprouts for 10–15 minutes until soft. Steam the sweet potatoes for 8–10 minutes until soft. Tip them both into a bowl and mash together.

Heat half the oil or butter in a frying pan. Add the garlic and cook for a few minutes, then stir it into the mash along with the nutmeg, toasted hazelnuts, salt and pepper.

Heat the rest of the oil or butter in the frying pan and dollop the mash back in.

Press down the mash with the back of a spoon and leave to cook for a few minutes, undisturbed, to get a crispy underside.

Once the underside has started to brown, flip it over. Don't worry if it breaks up a bit, just flip over each piece. Cook for a few minutes until crispy on the bottom.

Serve with vegetarian sausages for Sunday brunch or with soured cream for a light supper.

Cheddar and Courgette Frittata

With just a few basic ingredients, this frittata is quick and easy to make. In place of courgettes, try mushrooms, spinach or tomatoes. Cooked purple-sprouting broccoli also works well. The frittata can be made in advance and stored, wrapped, in the fridge. Remove from the fridge an hour before serving to bring it to room temperature.

GF

Serves 4

2 tbsp butter
1 onion, finely chopped
3 courgettes, sliced
8 eggs
85g/3oz Cheddar cheese, grated
sea salt and freshly ground
   black pepper

To serve
potato salad and a fresh green salad

Heat the butter in a heavy-based frying pan and add the onion. Fry for 10 minutes, stirring occasionally, until soft but not browned.

Add the courgettes and cook for about 10 minutes until soft.

Beat the eggs in a bowl and season with a little salt and pepper.

Add the eggs to the onion and courgette mixture and cook until the base has set, tipping the pan so the uncooked egg runs underneath.

Sprinkle the cheese on top and cook under a medium-hot grill for about 10 minutes until the cheese is beginning to brown and bubble. Leave to settle for 10 minutes before serving.

Serve warm or cool with a potato salad and fresh green leaves.

Mushroom and Tofu-filled Chinese Pancakes

Chinese pancakes are often served with crispy duck but vegetable fillings work just as well. Feel free to use any type of mushroom or other vegetables. The combination of cooked vegetables, fresh, crispy lettuce leaves and cucumber strips brings a pleasing range of textures. Honey, maple syrup or sugar can be added during the cooking if you want a caramelised flavour.

DF V

Serves 4 as a starter or side dish or 2 as a main course

2 tbsp olive oil
225g/8oz chestnut mushrooms, sliced
225g/8oz smoked or marinated tofu, cubed
1 tbsp tamari soy sauce
1 tsp toasted sesame oil
1 tbsp rice wine (optional)
6 Chinese pancakes
1 little gem lettuce, separated into leaves
¼ cucumber, cut into thin strips
4 tbsp hoisin sauce

Heat the oil in a frying pan. Add the mushrooms, tofu, tamari, toasted sesame oil and rice wine and cook until the mushrooms are cooked and the sauce is beginning to thicken.

Steam the pancakes or cook according to the instructions on the packet.

Put the mushroom mixture, lettuce, cucumber and hoisin sauce onto separate dishes.

Spread each pancake with some hoisin sauce and a lettuce leaf and top with mushrooms and cucumber. Fold the pancake over and enjoy.

Aubergine Roll-ups

This dish can be served as a starter or light lunch. There are many fillings that would work just as well as those listed here, so feel free to be creative and adapt it to your own tastes and what's in the fridge. Nut or seed butters, such as almond butter or tahini, can be used instead of the ricotta for a dairy-free, vegan roll-up.

DF* GF V*

Serves 4 as a starter or 2 as a main course

2 aubergines
2 tbsp olive oil
150g/5oz ricotta cheese (optional)
2 garlic cloves, finely chopped
2 heaped tbsp pesto
50g/2oz sundried tomatoes in oil,
  cut into strips
a few rocket leaves

To serve
toast or pitta bread

Remove the top from the aubergines, then slice them lengthways into 1cm/½in slices. Brush each slice with olive oil on both sides.

Grill the aubergine slices under a medium-hot grill for a few minutes on each side until they have softened. Transfer to a plate.

Mix the ricotta cheese with the garlic, then loosely swirl in the pesto. Spread most of the mixture over the aubergine slices and put the remainder in a bowl.

Lay slices of sundried tomatoes and a few rocket leaves on to each aubergine slice, then roll them up. Secure with cocktail sticks, if necessary.

Serve with toast or pitta bread.

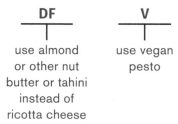

DF	V
use almond or other nut butter or tahini instead of ricotta cheese	use vegan pesto

Griddled Vegetables and Halloumi with Basil Dressing

Using a griddle pan to cook the vegetables and halloumi gives a pleasing appearance and a range of flavours. However, if you don't have a griddle pan, use the grill or a heavy-based frying pan. Other examples of vegetables that could be used in this dish include mushrooms, peppers, red onions and asparagus.

DF* GF V*

Serves 4 as a starter or side dish or 2 as a main course

1 aubergine
2 courgettes
1 sweet potato, peeled
3 tbsp olive oil
150g/5oz halloumi cheese, thinly sliced
225g/8oz cherry tomatoes, halved (optional)
1 tbsp lemon juice
a large bunch of basil, torn into pieces

Remove the top from the aubergine and slice at an angle to create thin ovoid-shaped pieces. Top and tail the courgettes and slice at an angle into thin slices. Slice the sweet potato into thin rounds.

Brush both sides of the aubergine, courgette and sweet potato slices with a little of the olive oil.

Heat the griddle pan and cook the vegetables for 5 minutes on each side in batches. As each batch is cooked, transfer them to a plate, then continue until all the vegetables are cooked.

Next, griddle the halloumi for about 5 minutes on each side until lightly browned, then finally griddle the cherry tomatoes, if using, which will only need a minute.

Blitz together the remaining olive oil with the lemon juice and basil leaves to make the dressing.

Combine the vegetables and halloumi in a bowl and drizzle with the basil dressing.

DF V

use tofu or tempeh instead of halloumi

Soups

On a chilly day, what could be more comforting
than a hearty, homemade soup served with crusty
bread and salty butter. The soups in this section
are all fairly substantial, so served with a roll
and salad can constitute a meal in themselves.
Alternatively, they can be served as a starter. It's
worth making double the amount you need so that
leftovers can be enjoyed the next day. There is a lot
of flexibility in terms of which vegetables or pulses
are added, so use these recipes as a springboard
from which to create your own variations.

Spicy Sweet Potato and Cannellini Bean Soup

The sweet potatoes give this soup a creamy sweetness and bright colour. The cannellini beans provide protein, fibre and texture, while spices add to the warming nature of the soup. If you prefer, you can used dried beans instead of the canned version. Soak 85g/3oz dried cannellini beans overnight in cold water, drain, then boil in fresh water for about 1 hour until soft to use.

DF GF V

Serves 4

2 tbsp olive oil
1 red onion, finely chopped
2 tsp finely chopped root ginger
a pinch of cayenne pepper
450g/1lb sweet potatoes, peeled
  and cut into large chunks
600ml/1 pint water, plus extra to adjust
  consistency
400g/14oz can cannellini
  beans, drained
2 tsp creamed coconut (optional)
½ tsp paprika or freshly grated nutmeg
3 tbsp cream or Cashew Cream
  (see page 157)
sea salt and freshly ground
  black pepper

To serve
crusty bread and a green salad (optional)

Heat the oil in a large pan and sauté the onion for a few minutes until soft but not browned.

Add the ginger and cayenne pepper and cook for a few minutes, stirring.

Stir in the sweet potatoes. Add the water, bring to the boil, then reduce the heat, cover and simmer for 10–15 minutes until the sweet potatoes are soft.

Add the cannellini beans and cook for a few more minutes until blended and heated through.

Stir in the creamed coconut, if using.

Blend the soup with a hand blender or in a liquidiser until smooth, then add enough boiling water to make the desired consistency.

Season with salt and pepper to taste, then swirl in a little cream or cashew cream, sprinkle with paprika or grated nutmeg and serve with crusty bread and a green salad, if you like.

Cauliflower and Cashew Nut Soup

The cashew nuts in this recipe add depth of flavour and creaminess as well as making the soup both filling and nutritious. The cauliflower can be replaced with root vegetables such as carrots, squash or parsnips, if you like, which will give the soup a sweeter taste.

DF* GF V

Serves 4

3 tbsp olive oil or butter
2 tsp finely chopped root ginger
1 large cauliflower, cut into florets
4 tbsp cashew-nut butter
2 tbsp chopped coriander
3 tbsp cashew nuts, toasted
  (see page 24)
sea salt or rock salt

Heat 2 tablespoons oil or butter in a saucepan and sauté the ginger for a few minutes.

Reserve a few small cauliflower florets and add the remainder to the pan. Cook for a few minutes, stirring well so it is coated in the flavoured oil.

Add just enough water to cover the vegetables, bring to the boil, then reduce the heat, cover and simmer for 10–15 minutes until the cauliflower is soft.

Meanwhile, heat the remaining oil in a small frying pan and fry the reserved cauliflower florets until lightly browned.

Stir the cashew-nut butter into the soup and season with salt to taste.

Blend with a hand blender or in a liquidiser until smooth.

Sprinkle the soup with toasted cashew nuts, fried cauliflower florets and chopped coriander just before serving.

DF

use olive oil

Minty Pea Soup

It's worth keeping a bag of frozen peas in the freezer so you can rustle up this soup for a quick lunch. It takes only minutes to make and is delicious. The bright green colour is pleasing to the eye and the sweet taste appeals to people of all ages. If you are really short of time, leave out the spring onions.

DF* GF V

Serves 4

2 tbsp butter or olive oil
5 spring onions, chopped
   (optional)
300g/10oz frozen peas
750ml/1¼ pint boiling water
2 tbsp chopped mint
4 tbsp crème fraîche or natural
   yogurt (optional)
sea salt and freshly ground
   black pepper

Heat the butter or oil in a saucepan, add the spring onions and cook gently for a few minutes until they are soft but not browned.

Add the frozen peas and boiling water. Bring to the boil, then reduce the heat, cover and simmer for about 5 minutes until everything is thoroughly hot and well blended.

Add the mint, season with salt and pepper to taste, and blend with a hand blender or in a liquidiser until smooth.

Serve with a swirl of crème fraîche or yogurt in each bowl.

DF

use olive oil
and soya yogurt

Sweetcorn Chowder

Sweetcorn makes a good base for a chowder, providing sweetness and colour, while the potatoes give the finished dish a thick and creamy texture. This recipe uses frozen or canned sweetcorn but you can use fresh corn cut from the cob when it is in season.

DF GF V

Serves 4

50g/2oz butter or 3 tbsp olive oil
1 garlic clove, finely chopped
150g/5oz potatoes, cut into
  2cm/¾in cubes
600ml/1 pint hot vegetable stock
  or water
200g/7oz frozen or canned,
  drained sweetcorn
50ml/2fl oz double cream or
  soya yogurt
2 tbsp finely chopped parsley
sea salt and freshly ground
  black pepper

Heat the butter or oil in a saucepan and sauté the garlic for a minute.

Add the potatoes, stir and cook for a couple of minutes until well coated in the oil.

Add the hot stock or water, bring to the boil, then reduce the heat, cover and simmer for 10–15 minutes until the potatoes are soft.

Add two-thirds of the sweetcorn and cook for a few minutes until the sweetcorn has softened and is heated through.

Blend the soup with a hand blender or in a liquidiser. Stir in the rest of the sweetcorn with the cream or yogurt. Season with salt and pepper to taste and reheat gently.

Sprinkle with chopped parsley before serving.

Quinoa and Vegetable Soup

This is a chunky and filling soup that can be a meal in itself. For culinary purposes, quinoa can be used like other grains but it has the advantage of containing all the essential amino acids needed for bodily function, making it a good plant source of protein. Any vegetables can be used, so choose whatever is in season.

DF GF V

Serves 4

2 tbsp olive oil
2 tsp finely chopped root ginger
2 garlic cloves, finely diced
2 celery sticks, finely sliced
2 carrots, diced
2 courgettes, diced
200g/7oz French beans, sliced into
  2cm/¾in pieces
110g/4oz quinoa
1.5l/2½ pints hot vegetable stock
  or water
2 tsp dried thyme
400g/14oz can chopped tomatoes
200g/7oz kale, ribs removed and
  chopped
a handful of basil leaves (optional)
sea salt and freshly ground
  black pepper

In a large pan, heat the olive oil and sauté the ginger for 2 minutes. Add the garlic and cook for a further minute.

Add the celery, carrots, courgettes, green beans and quinoa and stir to coat all the ingredients with oil.

Add the hot stock or water, the thyme and tomatoes and bring to the boil. Reduce the heat, cover and simmer for 15 minutes until the vegetables are tender.

Add the kale and season with salt and pepper to taste. Cover and cook for a few minutes until the kale has wilted.

Tear in the basil leaves, if using, just before serving.

Lentil, Vegetable and Coconut Soup

Any seasonal vegetables can be used in this soup. Alternatives to those listed include sweet potatoes, white potatoes, turnips, squash, courgettes, green beans, runner beans, cauliflower and beetroot. Soaking the lentils makes them easier to digest and reduces the cooking time but is not essential.

DF GF V

Serves 4

2 tbsp olive oil
1 large onion, chopped
2 tsp chopped root ginger
150g/5oz Puy lentils, preferably
  soaked for a few hours
900ml/1½ pints vegetable stock
  or water
½ celeriac or swede, peeled
  and chopped
2 parsnips, peeled and chopped
2 carrots, sliced
2 tsp dried mixed herbs
200g/7oz kale, stems removed
  and leaves chopped
2 tbsp creamed coconut
2 tbsp tamari soy sauce
sea salt and freshly ground
  black pepper

Heat the oil in a large saucepan and fry the onion for a few minutes until soft but not browned, stirring occasionally. Add the ginger and cook for a few more minutes.

Drain and rinse the lentils and add them to the onions along with the vegetable stock or water. Bring to the boil, skim off any scum that rises to the surface, then reduce the heat and simmer for 20 minutes.

Add all the root vegetables to the pan with the mixed herbs. Return the soup to the boil, then cover and simmer for about 15 minutes until the vegetables are tender. Add the kale and cook for a few more minutes until wilted.

Stir in the creamed coconut and tamari. Season with salt and pepper to taste and stir well to melt the coconut into the soup before serving.

Miso Noodle Soup

Miso is a paste made from fermented soya beans, and sometimes rice or barley. It is widely used as a source of umami in Japan. Umami describes a savoury deliciousness that adds depth of flavour to soups, stews and casseroles. Being fermented, miso is also considered to be a good digestive aid. There are many different types of miso, ranging in colour from light brown to very dark. In general, the lighter the miso the sweeter and milder it will taste. It is best to add miso towards the end of cooking in order to preserve its beneficial properties. This is a fresh-tasting, zingy soup that can be rustled up in 15 minutes.

DF GF V

Serves 4

4 spring onions, finely sliced
1 red chilli, deseeded and chopped
1 tsp finely chopped root ginger
1.5 litres/2½ pints water
300g/10oz buckwheat or rice noodles
6 shiitake mushrooms, sliced
2 carrots, cut into fine batons
2 heads of pak choi, stems separated
  from the leaves and sliced
2 tbsp miso paste
2 tbsp finely chopped coriander

Put the spring onions, chilli and ginger into a pan with the water, bring to the boil and simmer for a couple of minutes.

Add the noodles, mushrooms, carrots and the white stems of the pak choi. Return to a simmer and simmer until the noodles are just cooked. The time will vary according to the type of noodles you use, so check the cooking instructions on the packet.

Add the green leaves from the pak choi. Remove a few spoonfuls of water from the soup and mix it with the miso paste to thin it down, then stir the mixture back into the pan. Simmer for a minute until the pak choi is just wilted.

Garnish with the coriander and serve.

Broccoli and Butter Bean Soup with Toasted Almonds

The butter beans in this soup break down slightly to give a thick, creamy texture. Haricot beans or cannellini beans can also be used. The toasted, flaked almonds add a nutty crunch that outdoes croûtons any day.

DF GF V

Serves 4

2 tbsp olive oil
1 onion, finely chopped
1 large head of broccoli, cut into florets
2 x 400g/14oz cans butter beans, drained
600ml/1 pint vegetable stock
2 tbsp tamari soy sauce
4 tbsp flaked almonds, toasted (see page 24)
sea salt and freshly ground black pepper

Heat the oil in a saucepan, add the onion and cook for a few minutes until soft.

Add the broccoli, beans and stock, then pour in enough water to just cover the ingredients. Bring to the boil, then reduce the heat, cover and simmer for about 5 minutes until the broccoli is just soft.

Add the tamari to the soup and season with salt and pepper to taste. Spoon into bowls and sprinkle with toasted almonds just before serving.

Hearty Barley and Vegetable Soup

This nutritious soup is full of flavour and goodness and will leave you feeling thoroughly satisfied. The barley adds a chewy texture and thickness to the soup. Any vegetables can be used so go with whatever is in season and available. The soup also works well cooked in a slow cooker or in a low oven for a few hours.

DF V WF

Serves 4

3 tbsp olive oil or coconut oil
1 leek, sliced
2 celery sticks, finely sliced
110g/4oz pearl barley
2 bay leaves
2 tsp dried mixed herbs
1.2 litres/2 pints vegetable stock
  or water
2 carrots, diced
2 parsnips, peeled and diced
110g/4oz green beans, topped
  and tailed and sliced into
  2cm/¾in lengths
2 tbsp tamari soy sauce
sea salt and freshly ground
  black pepper

Heat the oil in a large pan, add the leek and celery and cook for a few minutes until they begin to soften.

Add the pearl barley, bay leaves and mixed herbs and stir to coat the ingredients in the oil.

Add the stock or water and bring to the boil, then cover and simmer for 30 minutes.

Add the carrots, parsnips and green beans, and season with salt and pepper. Cover and continue to simmer for 15 minutes until the vegetables are soft.

Stir in the tamari, cover and leave to sit for about 10 minutes before serving.

Tuscan Bean Soup

This hearty soup can be a meal in itself at any time of year, so use whatever vegetables are in season. Despite being extremely comforting, it is also highly nutritious so make plenty – you'll be glad of a second helping or leftovers the next day. If you're feeling indulgent, grate some Parmesan cheese onto the soup just before serving.

DF GF V

Serves 4

3 tbsp olive oil
1 red onion, finely diced
2 garlic cloves, diced
2 carrots, diced
2 celery sticks, finely sliced
2 courgettes, sliced
½ savoy cabbage, finely shredded
2 rosemary sprigs
2 bay leaves
2 x 400g/14oz cans borlotti beans, drained
2 tbsp tomato purée
1 litre/1¾ pint vegetable stock or water
sea salt and freshly ground black pepper

Heat the oil in a large pan and fry the onion for a few minutes until soft.

Add the garlic, carrots, celery, courgettes and cabbage and cook very gently over a low heat for 5 minutes, stirring occasionally.

Add the rosemary, bay leaves, beans, tomato purée and vegetable stock or water. Bring to the boil, cover and simmer for 20 minutes until the vegetables are tender.

Season with salt and pepper to taste. Remove the bay leaves and rosemary before serving.

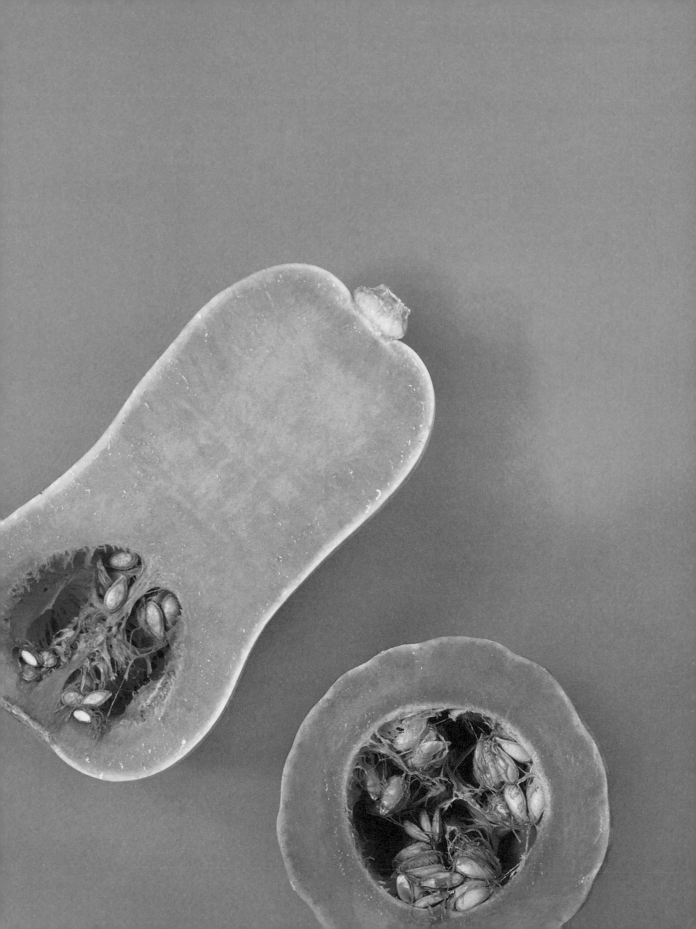

Main Meals

Whether cooking for yourself, your family,
friends or a celebration, the main meal of the day
is something to savour and enjoy. The meals in
this section are designed to cover a broad range
of occasions and appetites. There are plenty of
simple, inexpensive meals for everyday comfort.
For occasions when you want something a little
more glamorous, there are recipes that involve a bit
more time and preparation, but all are ultimately
designed to be achievable by even the novice cook.
They are proof – if proof were needed – that food
doesn't need to be complicated in order to be both
comforting and delicious.

Chickpea and Hazelnut Falafel

These can be served as burgers in a bun with tomato sauce or in pitta bread with rocket and tahini sauce. The falafel can be made in advance and kept in the fridge before cooking. They can also be pan-fried instead of baked. If you prefer, you can use dried chickpeas instead of canned chickpeas. Soak 175g/6oz dried chickpeas overnight (or for 8–12 hours), then drain, rinse and re-cover with fresh water. Boil for at least 1 hour until tender.

DF* GF V

Serves 4

50g/2oz hazelnuts
2 x 400g/14oz cans chickpeas,
  drained and rinsed
2 carrots, finely grated
1 garlic clove, finely chopped
2 tbsp tahini
a handful of coriander,
  roughly chopped
1–2 tbsp tamari soy sauce
3 tbsp sesame seeds
1 tbsp olive oil (optional), for frying
sea salt and freshly ground
  black pepper

For the salad
1 little gem lettuce, shredded
8 cherry tomatoes, quartered
½ cucumber, diced
1 small red onion, sliced
4 tbsp natural yogurt or soya yogurt
a splash of lemon juice
2 tsp chopped mint

DF
use soya yogurt

Preheat the oven to 190°C/gas mark 5 and line a baking tray with baking parchment.

Spread the hazelnuts onto a baking tray and roast in the oven for 10 minutes until lightly browned and fragrant.

Put all the ingredients, except the hazelnuts and sesame seeds, in a food processor, adding salt and pepper to taste. Blend for 5–10 seconds until the mixture is a fairly coarse paste. Add the hazelnuts and blend briefly to mix. Remove the blade from the processor. Divide the mixture into eight small spheres, then flatten them slightly.

Spread the sesame seeds onto a plate and press each falafel into the seeds before placing them on the lined baking tray. Bake for 15–20 minutes, turning them halfway through cooking, until cooked through and browned on both sides. Alternatively, heat the oil in a frying pan and fry for about 10 minutes, turning once.

Mix together the lettuce, tomatoes, cucumber and onion. Stir together the yogurt, lemon juice and mint, then toss with the salad.

Pile the salad onto serving plates and top with the falafel to serve.

Courgette, Fennel, Potato and Feta Bake

The melting cubes of cheese in this oven-baked dish make it a little different from a traditional gratin dish – and totally irresistible. It is readily adaptable to whatever vegetables you like and have to hand, so instead of fennel and courgettes, you could opt for cauliflower, celeriac, broccoli or green beans. You could also substitute sweet potatoes for the ordinary potatoes.

EF GF

Serves 4

450g/1lb potatoes, scrubbed
  but not peeled
3 tbsp olive oil or butter
1 large onion, chopped
2–3 courgettes, sliced
1 fennel bulb, sliced
200g/7oz feta cheese, chopped
  into cubes
a handful of parsley, chopped
110g/4oz Cheddar cheese, grated
sea salt and freshly ground
  black pepper

To serve
a green salad or steamed
  green vegetables

Preheat the oven to 190°C/gas mark 5.

Chop the potatoes into bite-sized pieces. Steam for 10–15 minutes until just tender, then transfer to an ovenproof dish.

Meanwhile, heat the oil or butter in a pan. Add the onion and cook for a few minutes until soft but not browned. Add the courgettes and fennel, cover the pan and continue cooking for about 10 minutes until the vegetables are soft.

Spread the courgette mixture over the potatoes, then top with the feta cheese. Sprinkle with parsley and season with salt and pepper to taste. Stir to make sure the ingredients are well mixed. Sprinkle the grated cheese over the vegetables.

Bake in the oven for about 30 minutes, or until the cheese is starting to brown. Serve with a green salad or steamed green vegetables.

Vegan Courgette, Potato and Tahini Bake

This is a vegan version of the courgette, fennel, potato and feta bake. The tahini makes a good alternative to cheese, providing depth of flavour and creaminess, as well as being an excellent plant source of calcium. Again, any vegetables can be used in place of the courgettes so use what is in season or available.

DF GF V

Serves 4

3 tbsp olive oil, plus extra
    for greasing
450g/1lb potatoes, scrubbed
    but not peeled
1 onion, finely chopped
3 medium to large courgettes,
    sliced
3 tbsp tahini paste
1 tbsp tamari soy sauce
juice of 1 lemon
about 200ml/7fl oz water
sea salt and freshly ground
    black pepper

For the topping
85g/3oz rolled oats
3 tbsp olive oil
3 tbsp chopped hazelnuts

To serve
a green salad or steamed
    green vegetables

Preheat the oven to 190°C/gas mark 5 and oil an ovenproof dish.

Chop the potatoes into bite-size pieces and steam or boil until they are just soft. Drain, if necessary, and transfer to the prepared dish.

Heat the oil in a pan, add the onion and cook for a few minutes until the onion is soft but not browned.

Add the courgettes and stir to mix, then cover and cook for about 10 minutes until the courgettes are soft.

Transfer the courgette mixture to the ovenproof dish with the potatoes.

Combine the tahini paste, tamari, lemon juice and water, then add more water, if necessary, to create a sauce about the thickness of single cream. Pour this onto the vegetables and mix well. Season with salt and pepper to taste.

To make the topping, put the oats into a bowl and rub in the olive oil. Stir in the hazelnuts. Sprinkle the topping over the potato and courgette mixture.

Bake in the oven for 30 minutes until crisp on top.

Serve with a green salad or steamed green vegetables.

Wild Mushrooms in Tahini Sauce

Mushrooms provide texture and depth of flavour to this dish, making it a delicious vegetarian treat. Any mushrooms can be used, so choose whatever is in season. If fresh mushrooms aren't available, use dried mushrooms and rehydrate as instructed on the packet before proceeding with the recipe. It's best not to wash mushrooms as it makes them soggy; instead, clean them with a small brush or scrape off any dirt with a knife, if necessary.

DF*   GF   V*

Serves 2 as a main course or 4 as a starter

3 tbsp extra-virgin olive oil
  or butter
4 shallots or 2 onions,
  finely chopped
1 garlic clove, chopped
250g/9oz wild mushrooms
  such as chanterelles, girolles
  or ceps, cleaned and sliced
200ml/7fl oz soya or oat milk
3 tbsp tahini
1 tbsp lemon juice
1 tbsp tamari soy sauce
about 150ml/¼ pint water
a handful of fresh parsley,
  chopped
sea salt and freshly ground
  black pepper

To serve
crusty bread or toast

Melt the oil or butter in a heavy-based frying pan, add the shallots or onions and cook for a few minutes until soft but not browned.

Add the garlic and mushrooms and cook for a further 10 minutes, stirring occasionally.

In another saucepan, gently heat the soya or oat milk but do not allow it to boil. Turn off the heat and stir in the tahini, lemon juice and tamari. Stir well, adding enough water to create a creamy sauce.

Pour the sauce over the mushrooms and heat gently.

Season with salt and pepper to taste and sprinkle on the chopped parsley. Serve with crusty bread or toast.

DF   V

use olive oil

Red Dragon Pie with Polenta Topping

Red dragon is a Chinese name for aduki beans, which gives this dish its lovely name. It can be made with a mashed potato topping but the golden polenta used in this version makes it extra comforting! The squash can be replaced with carrots, sweet potatoes or mushrooms. You may like to add a few mixed herbs. It is important that the polenta is not ready too much before the aduki beans are cooked as it will set and be hard to spread. So if you are using quick-cook polenta, start cooking when you add the carrots to the beans and rice as it will take about 5 minutes once it has come to the boil. If you are using traditional polenta, it will take about 30 minutes, so start once the beans have been boiling for 30 minutes.

DF* GF V*

Serves 4–6

225g/8oz aduki beans, soaked
 for at least 8 hours or overnight
110g/4oz brown rice, soaked
 with the aduki beans
3 carrots, sliced
1 garlic clove, finely chopped
1 butternut squash, peeled
 and chopped into bite-sized pieces
2 tbsp olive oil
2 tbsp miso paste (optional)
sea salt and freshly ground
 black pepper

For the polenta topping
about 1 litre/1¾ pints water
2 tsp salt
225g/8oz polenta
50g/2oz butter or olive oil
110g/4oz Cheddar or Red Leicester
 cheese, grated
2 tsp paprika

To serve
a green salad or steamed
 green vegetables

Drain and rinse the aduki beans and rice. Put them in a pan and cover with fresh water. Bring to the boil and skim off any scum that rises to the surface. Turn down the heat, cover and simmer for about 50 minutes until both the beans and rice are tender.

Add the carrots, garlic and squash and season with salt and pepper. Add a little more water, if necessary, so the ingredients are just covered, and return to the boil. Reduce the heat, cover and simmer gently for about 15 minutes until the vegetables are cooked. The beans will have partially broken down, creating a thick sauce.

Meanwhile, boil the water for the polenta. For slow-cooking polenta this will be 4–5 times the amount of polenta but check the instructions on the packet. Add 2 tsp salt to the water and slowly pour the polenta into the boiling water, stirring all the time so that no lumps form. Return to a simmer and cook until the polenta is tender, stirring very frequently to prevent sticking and clumping. The cooking time will be about 5 minutes for quick-cook polenta or 30 for traditional polenta.

Preheat the oven to 190°C/gas mark 5.

Once the aduki beans and vegetables are cooked, turn off the heat. Remove a small amount of cooking liquid from the aduki beans and mix it with the olive oil and miso paste, if using. Stir the paste back into the aduki-bean mixture, then transfer the aduki-bean mixture to a large ovenproof dish.

Once the polenta is cooked, stir in the butter or olive oil and most of the grated cheese. Taste and add more salt, if necessary. Spread the polenta over the aduki bean mix, sprinkle with paprika and the remaining cheese and bake in the oven for 30–40 minutes until hot right through and golden on top.

Serve with a green salad or steamed green vegetables.

DF V

use olive oil, omit the cheese and add some poppy seeds or fresh herbs to the polenta

Chickpea and Vegetable Korma

This is a mildly spiced dish so it's a great introduction for those who aren't keen on very spicy food, as well as being popular with curry-lovers. Any available vegetables can be used. If you're cooking your chickpeas from scratch, you'll need 225g/8oz dried chickpeas, but it's worth cooking double the quantity and freezing half – you'll be thankful for them when you need to bulk up a soup or stew at a later date. The amount of creamed coconut can be adjusted according to taste.

DF GF V

Serves 4

3 tbsp coconut oil or olive oil
1 large onion, finely chopped
1 tsp cumin seeds
1 tsp coriander seeds
2 tsp finely chopped root ginger
1 garlic clove, finely chopped
1 tsp turmeric
¼ tsp cayenne pepper
200g/7oz green beans, cut into
   2cm/¾in lengths
1 cauliflower, cut into florets
3 sweet potatoes, peeled and
   chopped into large chunks
2 x 400g/14oz cans chickpeas,
   drained and rinsed
85–110g/3–4oz creamed coconut
1 tbsp chopped coriander

To serve
chapatis or brown rice and raita

Heat the oil in a large saucepan, add the onion and cook for a few minutes until soft but not browned.

In a separate heavy-based frying pan, dry-fry the cumin and coriander seeds until they start to pop, shaking the pan occasionally. As soon as they smell fragrant, tip them out of the pan to prevent them from burning. Grind them in a pestle and mortar.

Add the spices to the onion with the ginger, garlic, turmeric and cayenne and cook for a few more minutes.

Stir in the green beans, cauliflower and sweet potatoes and stir well to coat them in the spices.

Add the chickpeas and enough hot water to just cover the ingredients and then bring to the boil. Reduce the heat, cover and simmer for 20–30 minutes, or until the vegetables are cooked through.

Transfer some of the liquid from the pan into a bowl and stir in the creamed coconut until dissolved. Stir this back into the pan and cook for a few minutes.

Sprinkle over the fresh coriander just before serving with chapatis or brown rice and raita.

Lentil Dhal

This can be served with the Chickpea and Vegetable Korma (see page 71), or it can work as a meal on its own with rice, chapatis or naan bread. Soaking the lentils is not essential but it does reduce the cooking time and makes the lentils more digestible. Leftovers can be transformed into a soup with the addition of a little water, coconut milk or a tin of tomatoes.

DF GF V

Serves 4–6

300g/10oz red split lentils,
  preferably soaked for a few hours
600ml/1 pint water
2 tbsp olive oil, butter or ghee
1 onion, finely chopped
1–2 tsp cumin seeds
1–2 tsp coriander seeds
1 tsp mustard seeds
2–4 tsp chopped root ginger
1–2 tsp turmeric
¼ tsp cayenne pepper,
  or to taste
sea salt and freshly ground
  black pepper

Drain and rinse the lentils. Put them in a pan and cover with the water. Bring to the boil, then skim off any foam that rises to the surface. Turn down the heat, cover and simmer until tender and thick – about 25 minutes depending on whether or not they have been soaked. Add a little more water if the mixture is too dry or begins to stick to the pan. You are looking for a thick, dolloping consistency.

Meanwhile, heat the oil, butter or ghee in a pan and sauté the onion for a few minutes until soft but not browned.

In a separate heavy-based frying pan, dry-fry the cumin, coriander and mustard seeds until they start to pop, shaking the pan occasionally. As soon as they smell fragrant, tip them out of the pan to prevent them from burning. Grind them in a pestle and mortar.

Add the ground spices to the onions along with the ginger, turmeric and cayenne. Cook for a few minutes, stirring.

Once the lentils are cooked, stir in the onion and spice mix and continue to simmer gently. Season with salt and pepper to taste and cook for a further 10 minutes before serving.

Quinoa Pilaf

This can be served warm or cold and is perfect for a packed lunch or picnic. Alternative ingredients to add to the quinoa include mung bean or lentil sprouts, grated carrot or roasted vegetables.

DF GF V

Serves 4

225g/8oz quinoa
350ml/12fl oz water
50g/2oz sun-dried tomatoes in oil
1 head of broccoli, cut into florets
225g/8oz mangetout or sugar
  snap peas
2 tbsp hazelnuts
2 tbsp chopped coriander
sea salt and freshly ground
  black pepper

For the dressing
3 tbsp olive oil
1 tbsp lemon juice
2 tsp tamari soy sauce

To serve
mixed salad leaves (optional)

Preheat the oven to 200°C/gas mark 6.

Rinse the quinoa and put it in a pan, just cover with water and add a pinch of salt. Bring to the boil, then reduce the heat, cover and simmer until all the water has been absorbed – about 15 minutes.

Chop the sun-dried tomatoes.

Steam the broccoli florets and mangetout for a few minutes until just tender.

Toast the hazelnuts in the oven for 8 minutes until lightly browned.

Combine the cooked quinoa with the broccoli, mangetout, sun-dried tomatoes and hazelnuts in a large bowl.

Make the dressing by combining the oil, lemon juice and tamari. Gently stir this into the quinoa and vegetables.

Season with salt and pepper and sprinkle on the coriander. Serve on its own or with mixed salad leaves.

Cheesy Millet and Mushroom Bake

Many people think of millet as bird food but they've probably never tried this dish. Millet is a useful grain as it is gluten free, quick to cook and inexpensive, making it a good alternative to potatoes, pasta and rice. Instead of mushrooms, you could use sun-dried tomatoes or roasted aubergines. The recipe following this, on page 76, is a vegan version of this recipe.

GF

Serves 4

3 tbsp olive oil or butter, plus extra
   for greasing
1 onion, finely chopped
250g/9oz mushrooms, sliced
225g/8oz millet
750ml/1¼ pint water
3 eggs, beaten
110g/4oz Cheddar cheese, grated
2 tomatoes, sliced
sea salt and freshly ground
   black pepper

To serve
steamed green vegetables or
   a green salad

Preheat the oven 190°C/gas mark 5 and oil a shallow ovenproof dish.

Heat the oil or butter in a pan, add the onion and sauté for a few minutes until soft but not browned.

Add the mushrooms and cook for 10 minutes.

Meanwhile, put a dash of olive oil in a saucepan over a low heat and add the millet. Stir the millet to coat it in the oil and cook for a few minutes until it starts to smell nutty. Add the water and ½ tsp salt, bring to the boil, cover and simmer for about 15–20 minutes until all the water has been absorbed.

Season the beaten eggs with salt and pepper, then stir them into the cooked millet along with the mushrooms, onion and half the cheese. Transfer the millet to the prepared dish and sprinkle on the remaining cheese. Arrange the tomato slices on the top.

Bake in the oven for about 30–40 minutes or until set.

Serve with steamed green vegetables or a green salad.

Herby Millet and Mushroom Bake

This is a vegan version of the Cheesy Millet and Mushroom Bake (see page 74). Peanut butter can be used instead of tahini, if you prefer. You could also stir some toasted nuts (see page 24) into the millet to give a bit of crunch. If you use fresh rather than dried herbs, stir them into the millet once it is cooked.

DF GF V

Serves 4

3 tbsp olive oil, plus extra for greasing
1 onion, finely chopped
250g/9oz mushrooms, chopped
225g/8oz millet
750ml/1¼ pint water
2 tsp dried mixed herbs
3 tbsp tahini
1 tbsp tamari soy sauce
juice of 1 lemon
2 tbsp sunflower seeds
2 tomatoes, sliced
sea salt and freshly ground
   black pepper

To serve
a green salad or steamed
   green vegetables

Heat the oil in a pan and gently fry the onion for a few minutes until soft but not browned.

Add the mushrooms and cook for 10 minutes.

Meanwhile heat a dash of olive oil in a pan and add the millet. Stir the millet to coat it in the oil and cook for a few minutes. Add the water, herbs and ½ tsp salt, bring to the boil, cover and simmer until all the water has been absorbed – about 15–20 minutes.

Preheat the oven to 180°C/gas mark 4 and oil a shallow ovenproof dish.

Combine the tahini, tamari, lemon juice and enough water to create a pouring consistency.

Once the millet is cooked, combine it with the mushrooms, onion and tahini sauce. Season with salt and pepper to taste. Transfer the mixture to the prepared dish and sprinkle with the sunflower seeds. Top with the sliced tomatoes and bake in the oven for about 30 minutes until the sunflower seeds are just starting to colour and the tomatoes are sizzling.

Serve with a green salad or steamed green vegetables.

Buckwheat, Hazelnut and Mushroom Loaf

This provides a good alternative to a traditional nut roast. The nutty flavour of the buckwheat complements the hazelnuts nicely. Substitute courgettes for the mushrooms, if you prefer, although I find that this recipe often gets the thumbs up even from those who don't usually like mushrooms! Other nuts can be used in place of hazelnuts or you can use a mixture of nuts. It's also fine to use dried herbs if fresh aren't available.

DF GF V*

Serves 4

2 tbsp olive oil, plus extra
  for greasing
225g/8oz buckwheat
350ml/12fl oz water
225g/8oz flat portobello
  mushrooms
2–3 carrots, finely diced
225g/8oz hazelnuts
2–3 tbsp finely chopped herbs
  such as oregano, marjoram,
  thyme and parsley
2 eggs, beaten
sea salt and freshly ground
  black pepper

To serve
roasted vegetables and
  vegetarian gravy

V
___
replace the eggs
with 2 tbsp tahini
or peanut butter

Preheat the oven to 190°C/gas mark 5 and oil a 900g/2lb loaf tin.

Put the buckwheat and water in a pan, add a pinch of salt and bring to the boil. Reduce the heat, cover and simmer for about 10–15 minutes until all the water has been absorbed.

Meanwhile, heat the oil and fry the mushrooms and carrots gently for a few minutes until soft but not browned.

Blitz the hazelnuts in a food processor until well chopped.

Combine the vegetables, cooked buckwheat, chopped nuts and herbs, then stir in the eggs, if using. If you are making the vegan version, combine the tahini or peanut butter with some water to create a thick pouring consistency before stirring it into the buckwheat. Season with salt and pepper.

Transfer to the prepared loaf tin and bake in the oven for 30 minutes until set and just browning on top.

Serve with roasted vegetables and vegetarian gravy.

Smoky Vegetarian Goulash

The smoked paprika in this dish adds depth of flavour but it is fine to use sweet paprika if you prefer. The goulash can be cooked in a low oven or a slow cooker. The slow cooking allows the flavours to meld together beautifully. Cooking in advance and leaving for a few hours before reheating until piping hot also works well.

DF* GF V*

Serves 4

3 tbsp olive oil or butter
1 onion, finely chopped
1 tbsp smoked paprika
1 tbsp mild paprika
¼ tsp cayenne pepper
3 courgettes, sliced
2 aubergines, sliced
1 small cauliflower, cut into florets
400g/14oz can cannellini beans, drained
500g/1lb 2oz tomato passata
2 tbsp tomato purée
sea salt and freshly ground black pepper

To serve
rice, couscous or crusty bread
soured cream, crème fraîche or natural yogurt

Heat the oil or butter in a large saucepan and sauté the onion for a few minutes until soft but not browned.

Add the paprika and cayenne pepper and cook for a few more minutes. Stir in the courgettes and aubergines. Cook for 10–15 minutes, stirring every now and then.

Add the cauliflower florets, beans, passata, salt and pepper. Cover and simmer for about 20–30 minutes until the vegetables are tender. Season further, if necessary, and stir in the tomato purée.

Serve with rice, couscous or crusty bread with a dollop of soured cream, crème fraîche or natural yogurt.

DF V

use olive oil
and soya
yogurt

Vegetable Crumble

Some people are surprised to get a crumble for their main meal rather than dessert but they are never disappointed. The soft, sweet, flavoursome vegetable base, together with the crunchy topping, make the perfect combination of textures and flavours. Whilst this version contains both wheat and dairy, the vegan, gluten-free version is also delicious.

DF*   GF*   V*

Serves 4–6

For the filling
900g/2lb seasonal vegetables,
   such as courgettes, mushrooms,
   carrots, swede, parsnips, fennel,
   squash, turnips, green beans, celeriac,
   sweet potatoes, cauliflower, onions
3 tbsp olive oil or butter
1 tsp chopped root ginger (optional)
1 garlic clove, chopped
2 tbsp tamari soy sauce
400g/14oz can chopped tomatoes
120ml/4fl oz water
sea salt and freshly ground black pepper

For the topping
50g/2oz mixed nuts and seeds, chopped,
   such as sunflower seeds, pumpkin
   seeds, hazelnuts, almonds, Brazil nuts
85g/3oz plain wholemeal flour
85g/3oz oat flakes
110g/4oz butter or margarine, diced
110g/4oz Cheddar cheese, grated

To serve
steamed greens and tomato sauce

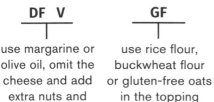

DF V	GF
use margarine or olive oil, omit the cheese and add extra nuts and seeds if you wish	use rice flour, buckwheat flour or gluten-free oats in the topping

Preheat the oven to 200°C/gas mark 6.

Chop the vegetables into largish bite-sized pieces.

Heat the oil or butter in a large pan, add the ginger and garlic and fry gently for a few minutes. Add the vegetables and stir well to coat in the oil.

Add the tamari, tomatoes and water, season with salt and pepper and bring to the boil. Reduce the heat, cover and simmer gently for about 10 minutes until the vegetables are soft. Stir intermittently and add a drop more water if it starts to dry out or stick.

Meanwhile, make the topping. Spread the nuts and seeds on a baking tray and toast in the oven for 10 minutes until just beginning to colour. Reduce the oven temperature to 180°C/gas mark 4.

Put the flour and oat flakes into a bowl and rub in the butter with your fingertips until you have a breadcrumb-like texture. Stir in the toasted nuts and seeds and the grated cheese.

Once the vegetables are cooked, transfer them to the ovenproof dish and spread the crumble mixture evenly over the top. Bake for 30 minutes until the cheese has melted and started to brown.

Serve with steamed greens and tomato sauce.

Polenta, Olive and Sundried Tomato Bake

Polenta has all the qualities of comfort food. It's soft and subtle but absorbs other flavours well – and being yellow, it even looks cheerful! The sun-dried tomatoes can be replaced with roasted peppers, courgettes or aubergines. Check the polenta packet instructions for both the quantity of water and the cooking time, as they will vary considerably depending on whether you have traditional or quick-cook polenta.

DF* GF

Serves 4–6

about 900ml/1½ pint water,
  but check packet instructions
1 tsp sea salt
200g/7oz coarse yellow polenta
2 tsp chopped thyme
110g/4oz sun-dried tomatoes,
  chopped
3 eggs, separated
1–2 tbsp butter or olive oil,
  plus extra for greasing
300g/10oz Cheddar or Red
  Leicester cheese, grated
10 pitted black olives
sea salt and freshly ground black pepper

To serve
a green salad or crunchy coleslaw

DF
replace the cheese with toasted chopped nuts (see page 24)

Bring the quantity of water specified on the polenta packet to the boil in a large pan with the salt. Slowly pour in the polenta, stirring all the time. Add the thyme and the sun-dried tomatoes. Cook on a low heat for as long as the instructions on the polenta packet indicate. It could be anywhere from 3 minutes for quick-cook polenta to 40 minutes for traditional polenta, stirring regularly to avoid clumping and sticking.

Preheat the oven to 180°C/gas mark 4 and grease an ovenproof dish.

While the polenta is cooking, whisk the egg whites until they form stiff peaks.

Once the polenta is cooked, turn off the heat and stir in the butter or olive oil with two-thirds of the cheese and the egg yolks. Season with black pepper and a little more salt, if necessary. Fold the egg whites carefully into the polenta mixture, then spoon the mixture evenly into the prepared dish and smooth the top. Sprinkle on the rest of the grated cheese and dot with the olives.

Bake in the oven for 40–50 minutes until set and beginning to brown.

Serve with a green salad or crunchy coleslaw.

Easy Cheesy Potato and Cauliflower Bake

This simple dish always goes down well with family groups as even the pickiest of eaters love it. Other vegetables can be added in place of the cauliflower – courgettes, mushrooms and green beans all work well.

GF

Serves 4

450g/1lb potatoes, scrubbed and chopped into bite-sized pieces (no need to peel)
1 cauliflower, cut into florets
3 tbsp olive oil or butter
1 onion, finely chopped
2 eggs, beaten
1 tbsp finely chopped chives (optional)
200g/7oz cheese, grated
1 tbsp paprika
sea salt and freshly ground black pepper

To serve
homemade tomato sauce and a green salad

Preheat the oven to 190°C/gas mark 5.

Boil or steam the potatoes for about 15 minutes and the cauliflower for about 10 minutes until just soft.

Heat the oil in a pan, add the onions and fry gently until soft but not browned.

Combine the potatoes and onions in an ovenproof dish. Stir in the beaten eggs. Add the chives, if using, and season with salt and pepper. Sprinkle the cheese on top, followed by the paprika.

Bake in the oven for 30–40 minutes until the egg has set and the cheese is bubbling and beginning to go golden brown.

Serve with homemade tomato sauce and a green salad.

Creamy Cannellini Beans

Don't be put off by the fact that this is vegan – it really is just as creamy as any dairy-based dish. Other beans that work well include borlotti beans, pinto beans or flageolet beans. It's mildly spiced, but if you want it spicier, simply add more cayenne pepper and ginger.

DF GF V

Serves 4

2 tbsp coconut oil or olive oil
1 tsp finely sliced root ginger
2 garlic cloves, finely chopped
a pinch of cayenne pepper
½ tsp turmeric
2 x 400g/14oz cans cannellini
  beans, drained
1 head of broccoli, cut into florets
240ml/8fl oz water
225g/8oz spinach, chopped
400g/14oz can coconut milk
2 tbsp concentrated tomato purée
2 tbsp chopped parsley
sea salt and freshly ground
  black pepper

To serve
couscous, boiled rice or millet

Heat the oil in a pan, add the ginger and cook for a couple of minutes before adding the garlic, cayenne and turmeric. Cook for a couple more minutes.

Add the cannellini beans, broccoli and water. Bring to the boil, then cover and simmer for about 5 minutes until the broccoli is just tender.

Add the spinach and coconut milk and cook for a couple of minutes until the spinach is just wilted.

Stir in the tomato purée and season with salt and pepper.

Sprinkle on the chopped parsley and serve with couscous, boiled rice or millet

Oven-baked Chickpea Ratatouille

This recipe can also be cooked in a pan on top of the stove or in a slow cooker. The chickpeas add protein and texture as they hold their shape. Other beans that work well include borlotti beans, kidney beans or pinto beans. This is a meal in itself but can be served with rice or crusty bread.

DF GF V

Serves 4

2 garlic cloves, peeled and sliced
1 aubergine, quartered and cut
  into 5mm/¼in thick slices
3 courgettes, sliced
2 red or yellow peppers, deseeded
  and sliced into strips
4 tbsp olive oil
450g/1lb tomatoes, chopped,
  or use a 400g/14oz can
  chopped tomatoes
2 x 400g/14oz cans of chickpeas,
  drained
1 tbsp thyme, de-stemmed
  and chopped
a bunch of basil
sea salt and freshly ground
  black pepper

Preheat the oven to 220°C/gas mark 7.

Put the garlic, aubergines, courgettes and peppers in an ovenproof dish and drizzle with olive oil. Mix well and roast in the oven for 30 minutes.

Turn down the oven to 170°C/gas mark 3. Remove the dish from the oven, add the tomatoes, chickpeas, thyme, salt and pepper and give the mix a good stir.

Cover with foil and cook for 40–60 minutes until the vegetables are soft.

Remove from the oven and tear in the basil before serving.

Sweet Potato, Lentil and Walnut Burgers

These can be served in the same way as any other type of burger. Try them in a bun with ketchup, in a pitta bread with guacamole or with a fresh green salad. For a barbecue flavour, add smoked paprika to the lentils. The burgers can be pan-fried but chill them first and handle them carefully as they may fall apart. Two beaten eggs can be added to help bind them but are not essential. The mixture can be made in advance and stored, covered, in the fridge until needed.

DF   GF*   V

Serves 4

175g/6oz red split lentils
450ml/¾ pint water
85g/3oz oat or buckwheat flakes
1 tsp dried oregano
1 tbsp olive oil
3 sweet potatoes, about 850g/1lb
  14oz, peeled and chopped
150g/5oz walnut pieces
sea salt and freshly ground
  black pepper

To serve
4 burger or brioche buns
a few lettuce leaves
2 sliced tomatoes
guacamole (see page 11)

Preheat the oven to 190°C/gas mark 5 and line a baking tray with baking parchment.

Rinse the lentils, put them in a pan with the water and bring to the boil. Skim off any scum that rises to the surface. Turn down the heat, cover and simmer for about 20–25 minutes until the lentils are soft and you have a thick lentil mixture.

Once the lentils are cooked, stir in the oat or buckwheat flakes, oregano and olive oil, then season with salt and pepper. Stir well, then leave to cool slightly.

Meanwhile, steam the sweet potatoes for about 15 minutes until soft. Mash them lightly and set aside to cool.

Spread the walnuts out on a baking tray and toast in the oven for 6 minutes until just crunchy.

Combine the sweet potato mash and walnuts with the lentils. Shape the mixture into 8–10 small burger-sized patties and place on the prepared baking tray. Smaller burgers are less likely to fall apart!

Bake in the oven for 20–25 minutes, turning them over halfway through cooking, until cooked through and crunchy on the outside. Serve the burgers in buns, if you like, with lettuce, tomatoes and guacamole.

GF

use gluten-free buns

91

Barley and Broad Bean Risotto

Barley has a nutty taste and chewy texture that makes a tasty and economical alternative to risotto rice in this dish. For a change, in place of broad beans try edamame beans or French green beans. If you use water instead of stock, add a glug of tamari soy sauce to add depth of flavour. If you don't have the patience to add the water bit by bit, you can add it all at once, then cover and simmer until it has been absorbed.

DF* WF V*

Serves 4

2 tbsp olive oil or butter
2 garlic cloves, chopped
225g/8oz pearl barley
600ml/1 pint hot vegetable stock
  or water
225g/8oz fresh or frozen
  broad beans
sea salt and freshly ground
  black pepper
2 tomatoes, chopped
juice of ½ lemon
2 tbsp chopped basil or coriander
50g/2oz Parmesan cheese, grated
  (optional)

To serve
Greek salad

Heat the olive oil or butter in a frying pan. Add the garlic and cook for a minute.

Rinse the barley and add it to the pan. Stir well to coat the barley in the oil. Add a ladle of hot stock or water, stir and cook until most of it has been absorbed, then add more. Continue until you have used up nearly all the stock. This should take about 20 minutes.

Stir in the broad beans and the last spoonful of stock or water. Cook for a few minutes until the beans are just tender. Season with salt and pepper.

Just before serving, add the chopped tomatoes, lemon juice, fresh herbs and grated Parmesan, if using. Serve with a Greek salad.

DF V

use olive oil and
replace the cheese
with toasted nuts
(see page 24)

Buckwheat-filled Cabbage Parcels

Stuffed vine leaves are a regular feature in Middle Eastern cookery but cabbage leaves work just as well and are available all year round, making them an accessible and inexpensive alternative. That said, feel free to use vine leaves if you have them. Rice or minced meat are commonly used as fillings but buckwheat has a soft texture and nutty flavour that works well. Of course, other grains, nuts and vegetables can also be used as fillings so go ahead and experiment!

DF* GF V*

Serves 4–6

1 savoy cabbage
350g/12oz buckwheat groats
1 tsp caraway seeds
1 tsp chopped thyme
450ml/15fl oz water
15g/½oz dried porcini mushrooms, soaked for at least 20 minutes in 300ml/10fl oz of water
2 tbsp chopped nuts, lightly toasted (see page 24)
sea salt and freshly ground black pepper
50g/2oz butter or olive oil, plus extra for greasing
500g/1lb 2oz passata
1 tbsp muscovado sugar (optional)
a handful of basil leaves
110g/4oz grated cheese or sunflower seeds
2 tbsp paprika

To serve
a range of salads, mezze style

Core the cabbage and place in a large pan of boiling water. Boil the cabbage for about 5 minutes, then turn off the heat and leave the cabbage to blanch in the water for at least 5 more minutes.

Transfer the cabbage to a colander and run under cold water to cool it down. Leave to drain.

Put the buckwheat in a pan with the caraway seeds, thyme and water and bring to the boil.

Add the mushrooms and their soaking liquor to the buckwheat. Cover and simmer until all the water has been absorbed – about 10–12 minutes.

Preheat the oven to 180°C/gas mark 4 and oil an ovenproof dish.

Stir the chopped nuts into the buckwheat and season with salt and pepper.

Shake any excess water off the cabbage and separate it into leaves. Cut out the large central stems from the cabbage. Put a few leaves in the base of an oiled oven dish. Spoon a small amount of the buckwheat mix onto one end of each cabbage leaf. Fold in the sides and roll up to create cabbage parcels. Place the parcels onto the oven dish, with the seams underneath, fitting them snugly together.

Heat the butter or oil in a pan. Add the passata and sugar and heat gently. Season with salt and pepper. Tear the basil leaves into the pan and stir to combine. Pour the sauce over the cabbage parcels and scatter the grated cheese or sunflower seeds over the top.

Sprinkle paprika on top, cover with foil then bake in the oven for 20 minutes. Remove the foil, turn up the oven to 200°C/gas mark 6 and cook for 10 more minutes or until the cheese has melted.

Serve mezze style with a rangle of salads.

DF V

use olive oil and
sunflower seeds

Spiced Chickpea, Potato and Spinach Pie

This lightly spiced pie can be served hot or cold. Sweet potatoes or squash can be used in place of the white potatoes. If you don't have all the different spices, it's fine to use a couple of tablespoons of curry powder instead of the individual ones listed.

DF V

Serves 4–6

900g/2lb potatoes, chopped
   into bite-sized pieces
2 tbsp olive oil, plus extra for
   brushing the pastry and greasing
1 red onion, finely chopped
2 garlic cloves, finely chopped
1 tsp grated root ginger
1 tsp mustard seeds
1 tsp ground coriander
1 tsp ground cumin
1 tsp turmeric
a pinch of cayenne pepper
225g/8oz spinach leaves,
   chopped
400g/14oz can chickpeas,
   drained and rinsed
juice of 1 lemon
2 tbsp chopped coriander
6 sheets of filo pastry
sea salt and freshly ground
   black pepper

Put the potatoes in a pan, add ½ tsp salt and just cover with water. Bring the water to the boil, turn down the heat, cover and simmer until the potatoes are tender – about 15 minutes.

Preheat the oven to 190°C/gas mark 5 and brush a 23cm/9in pie dish with a little oil.

Meanwhile, heat the oil in a frying pan. Add the onion and cook until soft. Then add the garlic and spices and cook for a few minutes.

Stir the spinach into the spice mixture and cook for a few minutes until the spinach has wilted and is coated in the seasoned oil.

Drain the potatoes, then return them to the pan, add the chickpeas, lemon juice and coriander, and season with salt and pepper. Mash the ingredients together briefly with a fork, but leave it fairly chunky. Add the spice and spinach mixture and stir well.

Line the prepared pie dish with a filo sheet. Brush the filo with olive oil and lay a second sheet on top at right angles. Brush this with olive oil then lay a third sheet of filo at 45 degrees. Lay the fourth sheet at 45 degrees to this and brush with oil. The pie dish should now be covered with filo pastry.

To serve
mint raita or a Waldorf Salad (see page 131)

Distribute the potato mixture over the filo pastry. Press it down lightly with a spoon.

Cover with a sheet of filo pastry and brush it with olive oil. Lay the last piece of filo pastry on top at right angles. Gently fold the overhanging pastry over the top of the pie and scrunch these pieces down. Brush the top of the pie with olive oil.

Bake in the oven for about 15 minutes until the pastry is crisp and golden.

Remove from the oven and leave to rest for 10–15 minutes before serving with a minty raita or Waldorf Salad.

Spring Garden Hazelnut Paella

The vegetables in this recipe are seasonal in spring but you can adapt it by substituting any seasonal vegetables – I've included some suggestions below. The freshest vegetables will be those you have grown yourself but farmers' markets, box schemes and farm shops are also excellent sources of seasonal, locally grown vegetables.

DF GF V

Serves 4

2 tbsp olive oil
2 garlic cloves, finely chopped
225g/8oz brown rice
550ml/19fl oz vegetable stock
110g/4oz purple sprouting or green tenderstem broccoli
85g/3oz asparagus, sliced into 2cm/¾in pieces
85g/3oz sugar snap peas
2 tbsp hazelnuts, toasted (see page 24)
a handful of rocket leaves
sea salt and freshly ground black pepper

Heat the oil in a pan and add the garlic. Cook for a couple of minutes, then add the brown rice and stir well.

Add the vegetable stock, bring to the boil, then turn the heat down and simmer for 30 minutes.

Add the purple sprouting broccoli, asparagus and sugar snap peas and cook for 10–15 minutes.

Stir in the hazelnuts and season with salt and pepper. Garnish with rocket leaves just before serving.

Summer Garden Paella
Try broccoli, courgettes and fresh peas. Garnish with rocket and fresh tomatoes.

Autumn Garden Paella
Broccoli, kale and squash are available in the autumn.

Chestnut and Chard en Croûte

This is a celebration meal perfect for autumn or winter festivities. Even though it feels like a real treat and looks extra special, it is surprisingly easy to make, particularly if you use ready-made pastry and vacuum-packed chestnuts, as suggested here. You can substitute other cheeses for the Roquefort, if you prefer. The filling mixture can be made a day in advance and stored, covered, in the fridge.

Serves 6

50g/2oz butter
2 leeks, finely sliced
225g/8oz Swiss chard or rainbow chard, stems pulled off and stems and leaves chopped separately
400g/14oz can chestnut purée
3 eggs, beaten
225g/8oz vacuum-packed chestnuts, roughly chopped
50g/2oz oat flakes
225g/8oz Roquefort cheese, diced
½ tsp freshly grated nutmeg
500g/1lb 2oz pack all-butter puff pastry
a handful of flour, for dusting
melted butter or a beaten egg, for glazing
sea salt and freshly ground black pepper

Heat the butter in a heavy-based pan and stir in the leeks. Add the chard stems and cook for a few minutes until soft, stirring occasionally to prevent them from sticking or burning.

Add the chopped chard leaves and cook briefly until the leaves have just wilted.

Transfer the leek and chard mixture to a bowl and stir in the chestnut purée. Add the beaten eggs, chopped chestnuts, oat flakes and cheese. Grate on the nutmeg and season with plenty of salt and pepper. Stir well to combine all the ingredients. Cover the bowl and refrigerate for an hour or more to allow the mixture to firm up.

Preheat the oven to 220°C/gas mark 7 and line a baking tray with baking parchment.

Lightly flour a work surface and roll out the pastry into a large rectangle about 30 × 38cm/12 × 15in. Brush round the edge of the pastry with melted butter or a beaten egg.

To serve
roasted vegetables and
  Hollandaise sauce

Spoon the chestnut mixture down the length of the pastry, leaving 3–4cm/1¼–1½in clear at each end. Tuck up the ends of the pastry, then lift up the sides and wrap them round the filling. Pinch the sides together to form a seal, trimming off any excess pastry from the ends. Decorate with the trimmings, cut into shapes or leaves and arranged over the join.

Brush the pastry with the rest of the butter or egg. Make a few holes in the pastry to allow steam to escape as it cooks, and sprinkle with a little salt and pepper. Place on the prepared baking tray and bake in the oven for about 40–50 minutes until the pastry is golden and crisp. Cover the top loosely with foil after 30 minutes if the pastry is browning too quickly.

Serve in slices with roasted vegetables and Hollandaise sauce.

Ricotta, Tomato and Olive Tart

Using ready-rolled puff pastry makes this tart quick and easy to prepare. Instead of ricotta cheese, you could spread tomato purée or pesto on the base. And, of course, there are endless variations on the toppings. Try caramelised onions, artichokes in oil, roasted courgettes or asparagus spears.

EF

Serves 4

320g/11oz sheet of all-butter puff pastry
2 tbsp olive oil or melted butter
250g/9oz ricotta cheese
300g/10oz tomatoes, sliced
a few basil leaves, torn into pieces
50g/2oz pitted black olives
85g/3oz crumbly cheese, such
  as Wensleydale
sea salt and freshly ground
  black pepper

To serve
crisp green salad

Preheat the oven to 200°C/gas mark 6 and line a baking sheet with baking parchment.

Lay the pastry sheet out on the baking parchment. Score a border around the edge of the pastry about 2cm/¾in from the edge, without cutting through the pastry, and prick the pastry all over the centre with a fork. Brush the pastry with half the oil or melted butter.

Spread the ricotta over the pastry within the border. Arrange the tomatoes on top, overlapping slightly as they will shrink when cooked. Scatter on the basil and olives and crumble on the cheese. Season with salt and pepper and drizzle the rest of the olive oil or melted butter over the top.

Bake in the oven for 30–35 minutes until the pastry is golden brown and the cheese has melted.

Serve with a crisp green salad.

Cheese and Asparagus Tartlets

This recipe can also be made as one large tart. Any vegetables can be used depending on personal taste or what's available, but UK-grown asparagus is delicious and available in May and June. This recipe uses wholemeal flour for the pastry, which gives it a richer flavour, but white flour can be used, or try half wholemeal and half white flour.

Serves 4

175g/6oz wholemeal flour,
  plus extra for dusting
85g/3oz butter, diced, plus extra
  for greasing
about 2 tbsp water
3 eggs, beaten
175g/6oz asparagus, tough
  ends removed
150ml/¼ pint single cream
50g/2oz blue cheese or goat's
  cheese, diced
sea salt and freshly ground
  black pepper

To serve
Crunchy Beetroot, Carrot and Walnut
  Salad (see page 130)

Preheat the oven to 180°C/gas mark 4 and grease or line four 10cm/4in flan tins with baking parchment.

Put the flour in a mixing bowl and rub in the butter with your fingertips until the mixture resembles fine breadcrumbs. Gradually add enough water to make a soft dough.

Transfer the dough to a floured surface and divide it into 4 equal pieces. Roll each piece into a circle slightly larger than the flan tins. Press each circle into a flan tin, making sure the pastry comes over the top of each tin as it will shrink slightly. Trim the edges and prick the bases all over with a fork. Chill for 10 minutes if you have time.

Bake the tart cases in the oven for 15 minutes. Remove from the oven and brush the pastry generously with some of the beaten egg. Return to the oven and bake for 5 more minutes until the egg is set. Remove the flan cases from the oven and turn it down to 170°C/gas mark 3.

Meanwhile, cut each asparagus spear in half or thirds to fit inside the flan cases. Steam for 5–8 minutes until just tender. Arrange a few pieces of asparagus inside each flan. Stir the cream into the remaining egg, season with salt and pepper and pour this into the flan tins. Dot with pieces of cheese.

Bake in the oven for 20–30 minutes until the egg has set. Leave to stand for 10 minutes, then serve with Crunchy Beetroot, Carrot and Walnut Salad.

Polenta Pizza

If you want to make your own pizza but are not keen on making yeasted pizza dough or need to avoid gluten, this is the pizza for you. Polenta is easy to cook and makes a tasty, soft-textured base. For extra flavour, cook the polenta in vegetable stock rather than water or add herbs or poppy seeds to the polenta during cooking. It is possible to buy quick-cook polenta, but the quantity of water and the cooking time will vary considerably so, if you use this, follow the instructions on the packet.

GF

Serves 4

1.5 litres/2½ pints water
2 tsp salt
225g/8oz polenta
1 tbsp butter
25g/1oz Parmesan cheese, grated
1 tbsp olive oil, plus extra for greasing
140g/4½oz can or tube concentrated tomato purée
1 tsp dried oregano
110g/4oz mozzarella cheese, torn into pieces
75g/2½oz mixed pitted olives
150g/5oz sundried tomatoes in oil
110g/4oz grilled artichokes in oil, halved
a few basil leaves
sea salt and freshly ground black pepper

To serve
a green salad

Put the water and salt into a medium saucepan and bring to the boil. Once boiling, slowly stir in the polenta. Keep stirring as you add the polenta to prevent clumping. Turn down the heat to low and cook the polenta for 45 minutes, stirring every few minutes. (The cooking time will be much shorter if you use quick-cook polenta.)

Preheat the oven to 220°C/gas mark 7 and oil a 30 × 25cm/12 × 9in Swiss roll tin or baking tray.

Once the polenta is cooked, stir in the butter and Parmesan until blended, and season with pepper.

Spoon the polenta into the prepared dish and smooth it out evenly, then leave it to cool and set.

Meanwhile, combine the tomato purée, oregano and olive oil in a bowl. Season with salt and pepper. Spread this mixture over the polenta, leaving a 2cm/¾in border. Distribute the mozzarella pieces, olives and sundried tomatoes over the pizza, then arrange the artichoke halves amongst the mozzarella.

Bake in the oven for 15 minutes or place under a medium grill until the cheese is melting.

Garnish with fresh basil and serve with a green salad.

Autumn Vegetable Cobbler

A warming vegetable-based dish that's perfect as the days draw in. The suggested vegetables are those that are in season in the autumn and winter. Check out your local farmer's market or farm shop for the freshest and tastiest varieties. At other times of year, substitute spring or summer vegetables for the autumn ones. The topping can be made with olive oil instead of butter and without the cheese for a vegan or dairy-free version. This dish is a meal in itself but you can serve it with a salad, if you like.

DF* V*

Serves 6

2 tbsp olive oil or butter
1 red onion, finely chopped
2 tbsp mild paprika
1 butternut squash, peeled, deseeded and cut into large cubes
4 carrots, sliced
2 parsnips, peeled and sliced
1 small swede, peeled and cut into chunks
2 x 400g/14oz cans borlotti beans, drained
500g/1lb 2oz passata
2 tbsp muscovado sugar (optional)
1 tbsp chopped oregano
1 tbsp chopped thyme
2 tbsp tomato purée
sea salt and freshly ground black pepper

Heat the oil or butter in a large pan, add the onion and fry for 10 minutes until soft but not browned.

Add the paprika, squash, carrots, parsnips and swede, stir well and cook for a few minutes.

Add the borlotti beans, passata, sugar and herbs, and season with salt and pepper.

Cover the pan with a lid and cook for about 15 minutes until the vegetables are tender. Stir in the tomato purée and add more seasoning if needed.

Meanwhile, preheat the oven to 200°C/gas mark 6 and make the topping.

Put the flour and salt in a mixing bowl and lightly rub in the butter with your fingertips until the mixture resembles breadcrumbs.

Add two-thirds of the grated cheese and the rosemary. Stir in enough water or milk to make a thick dough.

For the topping
175g/6oz self-raising flour,
  plus extra for dusting
½ tsp salt
85g/3oz butter, diced
110g/4oz cheese, grated
2 tsp finely chopped rosemary leaves
a few tbsp water or milk

To serve
lettuce and tomato salad

DF V

use olive oil, omit
the cheese and
brush the scones
with a little extra
oil before baking

Turn the dough out onto a floured surface and knead it lightly to ensure the ingredients are well mixed. Roll it into a circle about 2cm/¾in thick. Cut the dough into 5cm/2in scones with a cookie cutter, cup or knife, or simply cut the circle into wedges.

Transfer the cooked vegetable mixture to an ovenproof dish. Arrange the dough pieces on top, brush with a little milk and sprinkle with the remaining cheese.

Bake in the oven for 20–30 minutes until the topping is well risen and the cheese has melted.

Serve on its own or with a lettuce and tomato salad.

Almond, Aubergine and Cauliflower Balti

Balti actually refers to a type of two-handled cooking vessel but it's okay to cook this curry in any large cooking pot. The ground almonds help to thicken the dish and create a creamy texture while the whole almonds add crunch. Cauliflower is perfect for spicy dishes as it absorbs the colours and flavours of the spices while retaining its shape and texture. If the list of spices feels daunting, just use a good curry powder or curry paste instead.

DF*   GF   V*

Serves 4

2 tbsp olive oil or ghee
1 large onion, finely chopped
2 aubergines, halved lengthways
   and sliced into semi-circles
2 tsp finely chopped root ginger
2 tsp black mustard seeds
2 tsp cumin seeds
2 tsp coriander seeds
1 tsp turmeric
1 tsp cinnamon
2 garlic cloves, finely chopped
1 cauliflower, cut into florets
400g/14oz passata
400g/14oz can chickpeas,
   drained and rinsed
3 tbsp ground almonds
3 tbsp roughly chopped coriander
3 tbsp whole blanched almonds, toasted
   (see page 24)
sea salt and freshly ground
   black pepper

To serve
naan bread and natural yogurt

Heat the oil or ghee in a large pan, add the onion and cook for 10 minutes until soft but not browned.

Stir in the aubergines and ginger and cook for a few minutes.

Meanwhile, heat a heavy-based frying pan and add the mustard, cumin and coriander seeds. When they start to pop, tip them out and crush them in a pestle and mortar.

Put the crushed seeds into the pan with the aubergines and onions and add the turmeric, cinnamon and garlic. Cook for a few minutes.

Add the cauliflower, passata and chickpeas, and season with salt and pepper. Cover and leave to simmer for 15 minutes until the cauliflower has softened.

Stir in the ground almonds and chopped coriander and heat through. Add the toasted almonds just before serving.

Serve with naan bread and a dollop of yogurt.

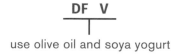

DF   V

use olive oil and soya yogurt

Cheesy Lentil Slice

This is made from store-cupboard basics so can be rustled up at any time. It holds together well so is perfect for buffets, packed lunches or picnics. For variety, add grated carrots, toasted walnuts (see page 24), or chopped chard. Serve hot with cooked vegetables and tomato sauce or cold with salads.

GF*

Serves 4–6

225g/8oz red split lentils, proferably soaked but this is not essential
450ml/¾ pint water
2 tbsp olive oil or butter, plus extra for greasing
1 onion, finely chopped
½ tsp cayenne pepper
110g/4oz Cheddar or Red Leicester cheese, grated
1 tsp mixed, dried herbs
1 egg, beaten
3 tbsp wholemeal breadcrumbs
sea salt and freshly ground black pepper

To serve
steamed green vegetables or a salad

Preheat the oven to 190°C/gas mark 5 and grease an ovenproof dish.

Drain and rinse the lentils and put them in a pan with the water. Bring to the boil, skimming off any scum that rises to the surface. Turn down the heat, cover and simmer for about 25 minutes until the lentils are soft and all the liquid had been absorbed.

Heat the oil or butter in a saucepan, add the onion and fry gently until soft but not browned. Stir in the cayenne pepper.

Combine the onion, lentils, cheese, herbs, egg and breadcrumbs. Season with salt and pepper. Transfer the mixture to the prepared dish and smooth the top. Bake in the oven for 30 minutes until set.

Serve warm with steamed green vegetables, or at room temperature with salad.

GF

use rye or gluten-free bread

Savoury Pancake Pie

This recipe involves making a batch of pancakes and then layering them up with delicious fillings between each pancake. Feel free to be creative in terms of what you use for fillings – anything goes. You can serve it on its own or with a range of salads in a picnic or buffet spread. Oh, and don't forget to make enough pancakes so you can make a sweet pancake pie as well! There are plenty of sweet fillings to choose from: jam, cream, lemon curd, berries, yogurt, maple syrup ...

Ideally, make the batter 30 minutes in advance to allow time for the starch to swell and the ingredients to meld together. In fact, you can make the pancake batter and fillings several hours, or even a day, in advance and store them, covered, in the fridge. Remove from the fridge 30 minutes or so before making the pancakes.

GF* DF*

Serves 4

For the pancake batter
110g/4oz plain flour
½ tsp salt
2 eggs, lightly beaten
300ml/½ pint milk
butter, coconut oil or olive oil,
  for frying and greasing

To make the batter, put the flour and salt into a bowl and make a small well in the centre. Add the eggs and begin to stir the mixture together, then gradually begin to add the milk, a little at a time, stirring continuously, until the mixture is smooth. If possible, leave to stand for 30 minutes.

Heat a heavy-based frying pan and add a small amount of butter or oil. When the oil is hot, whisk the batter thoroughly, then spoon a ladleful of it into the frying pan. Tilt the pan until the base of the pan is coated with a thin, even layer of batter. Cook for 1–2 minutes until the underside is lightly browned, then flip the pancake over and cook for a few minutes until the other side is golden. Transfer the pancake to a plate and keep warm. Repeat the process until all the batter has been used.

Preheat the oven to 170°C/gas mark 3, oil a flan tin and make or gather your fillings.

Filling ideas

mushrooms fried in butter or olive oil

cream cheese mixed to a spreading consistency with a little milk or lemon juice, and with chopped herbs, capers, grated horseradish or other flavourings stirred in

pesto

sun-dried tomatoes in oil

roasted courgettes or aubergines

pea purée, made by blending cooked peas with salt, water and a dash of olive oil (see page 22)

tahini or nut butter, thinned to a spreading consistency with a little water or lemon juice

grated cheese

Place one pancake in the base of the prepared flan tin. Spread one of the fillings on top, then lay on another pancake. Continue until your pie is as thick as you'd like it to be. It's fine to use the same filling twice or to make two shallower pies with different fillings in each. Brush the final pancake with oil and sprinkle on grated cheese, if you like.

Bake in the oven for about 10 minutes to warm through and melt the cheese, if necessary. The pie can also be served unheated.

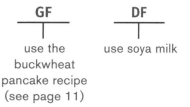

GF	DF
use the buckwheat pancake recipe (see page 11)	use soya milk

Filled Squash with Wild Rice and Hazelnuts

Any type of small squash can be used for this recipe. The principle is the same in that the cavity left by the seeds is filled with a delicious filling. Wild rice is expensive so often comes in a mix with other types of rice. Any of these mixes is fine to use here. Alternatively quinoa, millet, buckwheat or lentils could all replace the wild rice mix.

DF* GF V*

Serves 4

50g/2oz hazelnuts
2 squash, such as butternut, acorn,
  red kuri or sweet dumpling
2 tbsp olive oil
225g/8oz wild rice mix
50g/2oz Puy lentils
450ml/¾ pint water
2 tbsp goji berries or cranberries
110g/4oz cheese, grated (optional)
sea salt and freshly ground
  black pepper

To serve
crisp green salad

Preheat the oven to 200°C/gas mark 6.

Spread the hazelnuts on a baking tray and bake in the oven for 7–10 minutes until just starting to colour. Remove from the oven and roughly chop.

Halve the squash and scoop out the seeds. Put the squash halves into an ovenproof dish, cut-side up, and score the flesh with a knife. Drizzle with a little olive oil and season with salt and pepper.

Bake in the oven for 30–40 minutes until the squash is soft.

Meanwhile, put the wild rice mix, lentils and water in a pan with ½ tsp salt and bring to the boil. Turn down the heat, cover and simmer until all the water has been absorbed. If the wild rice is mixed with brown or red rice this will take about 40 minutes, otherwise check the instructions on the packet.

Stir the berries and hazelnuts into the cooked rice and lentils. Season with salt and pepper.

Spoon the rice mixture into the cavity of each squash. Drizzle with a little oil and sprinkle on the grated cheese, if using.

DF V

omit the
cheese

Return to the oven for 10–15 minutes until the cheese is bubbling. Serve with a crisp green salad.

Salads

The recipes in this section prove that some salads are substantial enough to be a comfort meal in their own right. Many work well in combination with recipes from other sections of the book to create a meal that satisfies every taste and texture sensation. The salads can also be combined with each other for a buffet or meze-style meal that everyone loves. One of the keys to delicious salads is the dressing, so stock up on lemons, mustard and good-quality oils, and grow fresh herbs on your windowsill.

Buckwheat, Pecan and Roasted Vegetable Salad

Don't be misled by its name – buckwheat is not related to wheat and is gluten-free, making it a good choice for those with wheat or gluten intolerances. Soft and easy to digest, it's a comforting food at any time of year. This recipe uses summer vegetables but you could make the dish with root vegetables instead in winter.

DF GF V

Serves 4

110g/4oz buckwheat groats
170ml/5½ fl oz water
2 aubergines
2 courgettes
3 tbsp olive oil
3 tbsp tamari soy sauce
110g/4oz shelled pecan nuts
4 tomatoes, chopped
1 tbsp lemon juice
sea salt and freshly ground
  black pepper

Preheat the oven to 220°C/gas mark 7.

Put the buckwheat and water in a pan with ½ teaspoon salt and bring to the boil. Cover and simmer for about 10–15 minutes until all the water has been absorbed.

Once cooked, transfer the buckwheat to a large salad bowl and leave to cool. Stand the bowl in a pan of iced water to speed the cooling process, if necessary.

Meanwhile, slice the aubergines lengthways into quarters and the courgettes lengthways in half, then slice both into 5mm/¼in thick slices and spread them out on a baking tray. Drizzle both with olive oil and tamari.

Roast in the oven for 20 minutes, then stir them around and return them to the oven for another 20–30 minutes until soft.

Towards the end of the cooking time, spread the pecans onto a baking tray and roast in the oven for 8 minutes until just crunchy.

When the aubergines and courgettes are cooked, transfer them to a bowl to cool.

Mix the cooled buckwheat, aubergines and courgettes with the tomatoes and pecans. Season with salt and pepper and drizzle on the lemon juice.

Red Rice and Edamame Salad

This colourful salad can brighten up any dinner table or lunch box. When tomatoes are in season use fresh ones, but sun-dried tomatoes add a nice chewy texture. Edamame beans are immature green soya beans that can be bought, frozen, from most supermarkets and some health-food stores. Rice should not sit at room temperature for too long so once it has cooled, cover it and put it in the fridge. Remove it from the fridge an hour before eating.

DF GF V

Serves 4

180g/6½oz red rice or red and
  white rice mix
450ml/¾ pint water
110g/4oz frozen edamame beans
  or broad beans
75g/2½oz sundried tomatoes
  or 2 tomatoes, chopped
75g/2½oz pitted black olives
75g/2½oz green olives
juice of ½ lemon
1 tbsp wholegrain mustard
2 tbsp olive oil
1 tbsp tamari soy sauce
2 tbsp chopped coriander
sea salt and freshly ground
  black pepper

Put the rice and water into a saucepan with ½ tsp salt and bring to the boil. Turn down the heat, cover and simmer until all the water has been absorbed. This will take about 30 minutes.

Transfer the rice to a salad bowl and stir in the edamame beans. The heat from the rice will be enough to cook them and they, in turn, will cool the rice.

If using sun-dried tomatoes, add them at this stage. If using fresh tomatoes, add them when the rice has cooled down – stand the bowl of rice in a pan of iced water to speed the cooling process, if necessary.

Once the rice has completely cooled, gently stir in the olives.

Mix the lemon juice with the mustard, then add the olive oil and tamari. Stir well, then drizzle over the rice. Season with salt and pepper and sprinkle on the coriander to serve.

Three-bean Salad

There are many different choices of beans when it comes to making a three-bean salad. The ones in this recipe have been chosen as they keep their shape better than some other beans, as well as for their contrasting colours. Using canned beans means this classic salad is incredibly quick to prepare, making it perfect to rustle up when you want to be healthy but don't have much time. If you are using dried beans, soak them for 8–12 hours, then rinse and cook in plenty of fresh boiling water for about 1 hour until soft. Pour on the dressing while the beans are still warm to allow the flavours to permeate.

DF GF V

Serves 6

400g/14oz can cannellini
  beans, drained
400g/14oz can kidney beans,
  drained
400g/14oz can black-eyed
  peas, drained
3 tomatoes, chopped into
  segments
2 large handfuls of rocket leaves
1 tbsp cider vinegar
1 tbsp wholegrain mustard
3 tbsp olive oil
sea salt and freshly ground
  black pepper

Combine the beans, tomatoes and rocket leaves in a large bowl.

Whisk together the vinegar and mustard in a jug. Add the olive oil and whisk again.

Drizzle the dressing over the salad and gently toss to combine all the ingredients. Season with salt and pepper.

Greek Salad

A lovely fresh salad that uses ingredients when they are at their most delicious and abundant in the summer months. Use any mixture of salad leaves you like – or just lettuce. Make sure the salad leaves and lettuce are completely dried after washing as the dressing will not stick to wet leaves and you'll have a puddle in the bottom of the bowl.

DF* GF V*

Serves 4

1 large lettuce, washed and dried
a handful of salad leaves, such as
  rocket, lamb's lettuce, mizuna
  (optional)
4 large plum tomatoes, halved and
  cut into segments
1 cucumber, quartered and sliced
110g/4oz pitted black olives
1 tbsp capers, rinsed if packed
  in salt
110g/4oz feta cheese, cut into
  1cm/½in cubes
a handful of basil
1 tbsp white wine vinegar
1 tbsp French mustard
4 tbsp olive oil
edible flowers to garnish, such
  as nasturtiums, calendula petals
  or borage flowers (optional)
sea salt and freshly ground black
  pepper

Tear the lettuce into bite-sized pieces into a large salad bowl and add the salad leaves. Add the tomatoes, cucumbers, olives, capers and feta and mix gently to combine the ingredients.

Tear the basil into the salad and season with plenty of salt and pepper. Gently stir the ingredients again.

Whisk together the vinegar, mustard and oil in a jug and pour it over the salad. Decorate with the edible flowers, if desired.

DF V

replace the feta with
toasted pistachios
(see page 24)

French Bean, Feta, Walnut and Beetroot Salad

A summery, richly coloured salad, this is perfect as a side dish or in a meze with other salads. Alternatively it's substantial enough to eat on its own for a light lunch. The feta can be omitted for a dairy-free version. The crunchy bitterness of the walnuts contrasts with the soft sweetness of the beetroot. To save time you can use ready-cooked beetroot or cook the beetroot the day before and store it in the fridge.

DF* GF V*

Serves 4–6

225g/8oz beetroot, washed
225g/8oz French beans, trimmed and cut into 2cm/¾in lengths
110g/4oz walnut halves
110g/4oz feta cheese, chopped into 1cm/½in cubes (optional)
1 tbsp balsamic vinegar
½ tbsp French mustard
3 tbsp olive oil
300g/10oz mixed salad leaves
sea salt and freshly ground black pepper

Put the beetroot in a pan with plenty of water and bring to the boil. Turn down the heat, cover and cook until the beetroot is just tender. This will take 50–60 minutes depending on the size of the beetroot.

Preheat the oven to 200°C/gas mark 6.

Drain the cooked beetroot, cool the beetroot under running water and slip off their skins. Chop them into bite-sized pieces and put them into a salad bowl.

Meanwhile steam the French beans for a few minutes until just tender. Rinse under cold water and drain well, then put in the salad bowl and leave to cool completely.

Spread the walnuts onto a baking tray and toast in the oven for 8 minutes until lightly browned and fragrant. Alternatively you can toss them in a dry frying pan.

Once the beans and beetroot are completely cool, add the feta cheese and toasted walnuts.

Make the dressing by whisking the vinegar and mustard together in a jug, then gradually whisking in the olive oil.

DF V

omit the cheese

Pour the dressing over the salad. Toss gently to coat all the ingredients in the dressing. Gently incorporate the salad leaves and season with salt and pepper to serve.

Sweet Potato, Sunflower Seed and Watercress Salad

Both sweet potatoes and watercress are rich in beta-carotene, the pre-cursor to vitamin A in the body. The sweet potatoes bring colour, sweetness and a comforting soft texture to this salad, while the watercress provides a welcome sharp contrast. The toasted seeds provide depth of flavour and crunch, and the yogurt dressing brings a creamy coolness.

DF* GF V*

Serves 4

4 medium sweet potatoes, peeled
  and chopped into bite-sized pieces
4 tbsp sunflower seeds
1 large bunch of watercress,
  stalks trimmed to make small sprigs
150g/5oz natural yogurt or
  soya yogurt
2 tsp wholegrain mustard
1 tsp white wine vinegar
sea salt and freshly ground
  black pepper

Preheat the oven to 200°C/gas mark 6.

Steam the sweet potatoes until just tender – this will take about 10 minutes. Once cooked, transfer the potatoes to a bowl and leave to cool.

Meanwhile, spread the sunflower seeds onto a baking tray and toast in the oven for 10 minutes until just starting to colour. Remove from the baking tray and leave to cool.

Combine the cooled sweet potatoes and sunflower seeds and gently mix in the watercress. Season with salt and pepper to taste.

Make the dressing by combining the yogurt and mustard in a jug, then stir in the vinegar.

Gently combine the dressing with the potato mix, or alternatively serve the salad onto plates and put a dollop of dressing on top.

DF V

use soya yogurt

Celeriac and Pumpkin Seed Salad with Almond Mayonnaise

Almond mayonnaise is easy to make and provides a creamy accompaniment to the crunchy celeriac but you can use other nut or seed butters or tahini, if you prefer. For a more colourful dish, include some grated carrots along with the grated celeriac.

DF GF V

Serves 4

4 tbsp almond butter
juice of 1 lemon
2 tbsp olive oil
½ tsp salt
3 tbsp pumpkin seeds
1 large celeriac
3 tbsp finely chopped parsley
sea salt and freshly ground
  black pepper

To make the mayonnaise, put the almond butter, lemon juice, olive oil and salt in a bowl and stir well to combine the ingredients. Add enough water to create a pouring consistency.

Toast the pumpkin seeds in a heavy-based frying pan until lightly browned and crunchy.

Coarsely grate the celeriac and mix it immediately with the almond mayonnaise. Do this quickly otherwise the celeriac will discolour. Stir in the pumpkin seeds and parsley and season with salt and pepper to taste.

Crunchy Beetroot, Carrot and Walnut Salad

Beetroots are usually eaten cooked but this salad makes the most of the earthy, crunchiness of raw beetroot. If totally raw beetroot doesn't appeal, try steaming the beetroots whole, with the skin on, for 15 minutes, then peel them before grating. This will soften the beetroot slightly but it will still retain a bit of crunch.

DF GF V

Serves 4

2 medium beetroots, peeled
3 carrots
2 tbsp walnut halves, toasted
  (see page 125)
2 tbsp chopped parsley
3 tbsp olive oil
1 tbsp apple cider vinegar
sea salt and freshly ground
  black pepper

Grate the beetroots and carrots and combine with the toasted walnuts and parsley in a bowl.

Mix the olive oil and vinegar together, then pour over the salad. Season with salt and pepper to taste and toss gently to combine the ingredients.

Waldorf Salad

The taste and texture sensations created by the combination of crisp celery, chewy raisins, crunchy walnuts, sweet red apples, tart green apples and creamy dressing provide both comfort and satisfaction. Soured cream or crème fraîche are both good alternatives to the yogurt and mayonnaise. The salad can be prepared in advance but it's best to add the walnuts just before serving so they retain their crunch.

GF

Serves 4

50g/2oz walnuts
2 celery sticks, finely sliced
1 red apple, cored and cut into
  1cm/½in pieces
1 green apple, cored and cut
  into 1cm/½in pieces
2 tbsp raisins (optional)
2 tbsp Greek yogurt
2 tbsp mayonnaise
sea salt and freshly ground
  black pepper

Preheat the oven to 200°C/gas mark 6.

Spread the walnuts onto a baking tray and toast in the oven for 8 minutes until just crunchy. Remove from the baking tray and leave to cool.

Combine the celery, apples and raisins, if using, in a bowl.

Stir the yogurt and mayonnaise together, then stir into the celery and apples. Add the walnuts and season with salt and pepper to taste.

Lemony Broad Bean and Artichoke Salad

This recipe uses frozen broad beans and artichokes marinated in oil to make it quick and easy. However, if you have fresh broad beans and artichokes, these can also be used. Peeled broad beans are a real treat but this step is not essential, especially if the broad beans are quite small. For a more substantial meal, add a can of cannellini beans or some crumbled feta.

DF GF V

Serves 4

200g/7oz rocket
450g/1lb frozen broad beans, thawed or cooked
8 artichoke hearts, marinated in oil
1 garlic clove, finely chopped (optional)
juice and zest of 1 lemon
2 tbsp olive oil
sea salt and freshly ground black pepper

Put the rocket into a large salad bowl. Slip the broad beans out of their shells, if you like, and add them to the rocket.

Slice up the artichoke hearts and add these along with the garlic, if using.

Sprinkle on the lemon zest followed by the lemon juice and olive oil. Season well with salt and pepper. Stir gently to combine the ingredients.

Bright Barley Salad

This colourful salad can be enjoyed at any time of year and is substantial enough to be a meal in itself. Pearl barley is used in this recipe but pot barley also works well. If you have vegetable stock use that, but water and bouillon powder can also be used. Using fresh corn sliced off the cob is delicious but canned or frozen corn tastes great.

DF WF V

Serves 4 as a starter or 8 as a side dish

225g/8oz pearl barley
600ml/1 pint vegetable stock or
  600ml/1 pint water and ½ tsp
  vegetable bouillon powder
200g/7oz sweetcorn
2 celery sticks, finely sliced
2 carrots, coarsely grated
3 tomatoes, finely chopped
4 tbsp olive oil
1 tbsp apple cider vinegar
1 tbsp finely chopped chives
sea salt and freshly ground
  black pepper

Rinse the barley and put it in a pan with the vegetable stock or the water and bouillon powder and bring to the boil. Turn down the heat, cover and simmer until soft and all the water has been absorbed. This will take about 50–60 minutes.

Once the barley is cooked, transfer it to a bowl and stir in the sweetcorn. The heat from the barley will cook or defrost the corn and the corn will help to cool the barley. Leave to cool completely.

Once the barley is cool, stir in the celery, carrots and tomatoes.

Make the salad dressing by combining the olive oil and cider vinegar. Drizzle the dressing onto the salad, sprinkle on the chives, season with salt and pepper and mix gently to combine the ingredients.

Green Bean and Avocado Salad

There's nothing better than a plate full of green foods to make you feel virtuous. Don't be fooled though, this salad is delicious and won't leave you feeling deprived. If you don't have all three types of beans, just use any that are available. Frozen broad beans make a quick and easy addition. Avocados are often best bought a few days before you want to use them so that they are properly ripe. Give them a very gentle squeeze – when ripe, they yield slightly under the pressure. The beans can be prepared in advance but add the avocado at the last minute to prevent browning.

DF GF V

Serves 4–6

200g/7oz mangetout or sugar
   snap peas, topped tailed and
   de-stringed
200g/7oz runner beans,
   topped, tailed and sliced into
   2cm/¾in lengths
200g/7oz French beans,
   topped, tailed and sliced into
   2cm/¾in lengths
1 tbsp French mustard
juice of 1 lemon
3 tbsp olive oil
1 garlic clove, finely chopped
   (optional)
1–2 ripe avocados
a handful of basil
sea salt and freshly ground
   black pepper

Steam the mangetout, runner beans and French beans until just tender – about 5 minutes. Refresh in cold water and drain well.

Make the dressing by whisking together the mustard and half the lemon juice, then stir in the olive oil.

Combine the cooked beans with the garlic and pour on the dressing. Mix well. If you are making this in advance, cover and refrigerate at this stage.

When you are ready to eat the salad, peel, stone and cube the avocado, sprinkle it with the remaining lemon juice, then add to the salad. Tear the basil leaves onto the salad, season with salt and pepper and fold the ingredients together.

Creamy Beetroot Salad

Sweet, earthy beetroots combined with the sharp creaminess of soured cream are a good route to the pleasure sensations in the brain. Chopped apples can be included for a bit of extra crunch. The horseradish gives a nice kick but is entirely optional.

DF* GF V*

Serves 4

300g/10oz beetroots, washed
200ml/7fl oz soured cream
1 tbsp cider vinegar
2 tbsp finely chopped chives
a pinch of grated horseradish
  (optional)
sea salt and freshly ground
  black pepper

Do not cut the ends off the beetroots before you cook them as this will cause them to bleed. Boil or steam the beetroot whole until soft – 40–60 minutes depending on their size.

Once cooked, run the beets under cold water or sit them in iced water until cool.

Trim them and slip off their skins – beware, you will get bright pink fingers! Cut the beetroot into bite-sized pieces and put in a salad bowl.

Once the beetroots are thoroughly cool, stir in the soured cream, cider vinegar, chives and horseradish, if using, and season with salt and pepper.

DF V

use natural soya yogurt instead of soured cream

Rainbow Salad

The vegetables in this recipe have been chosen for their bright colours but feel free to use any seasonal vegetables that you like. Butternut squash, beetroot, carrots, broccoli or steamed green beans can all be used to good effect. White quinoa is the most widely available but the recipe can also be made with red or black quinoa, which you can buy from some health-food shops. This salad is substantial enough to make a meal on its own but can also be served as a side dish.

DF GF V

Serves 4 as a main course or 8 as a side dish

2 red peppers, deseeded and
   cut into strips
1 large aubergine, cut into
   semi circles
2 courgettes, sliced into rounds
2 yellow squash, about 1kg/2lb 4oz,
   peeled and sliced
3 tbsp olive oil
2 tbsp tamari soy sauce
225g/8oz quinoa
450ml/¾ pint water
½ tsp salt
juice of 1 lemon
a few small sprigs of coriander
   (optional)
sea salt and freshly ground
   black pepper

Preheat the oven to 220°C/gas mark 7.

Spread the chopped vegetables onto baking trays and sprinkle with olive oil and tamari. Bake in the oven for 50–60 minutes, stirring halfway through.

Meanwhile, rinse the quinoa, put it in a pan with the water and salt, and bring to the boil. Turn down the heat, cover and simmer until all the water has been absorbed – about 15–20 minutes. When the quinoa is cooked, transfer it to a bowl and leave to cool.

Once the vegetables are cooked, remove them from the baking trays and leave to cool.

Combine the cooled quinoa, with the roasted vegetables in a large bowl. Sprinkle on the lemon juice and season with salt and pepper to taste. Serve sprinkled with the coriander sprigs.

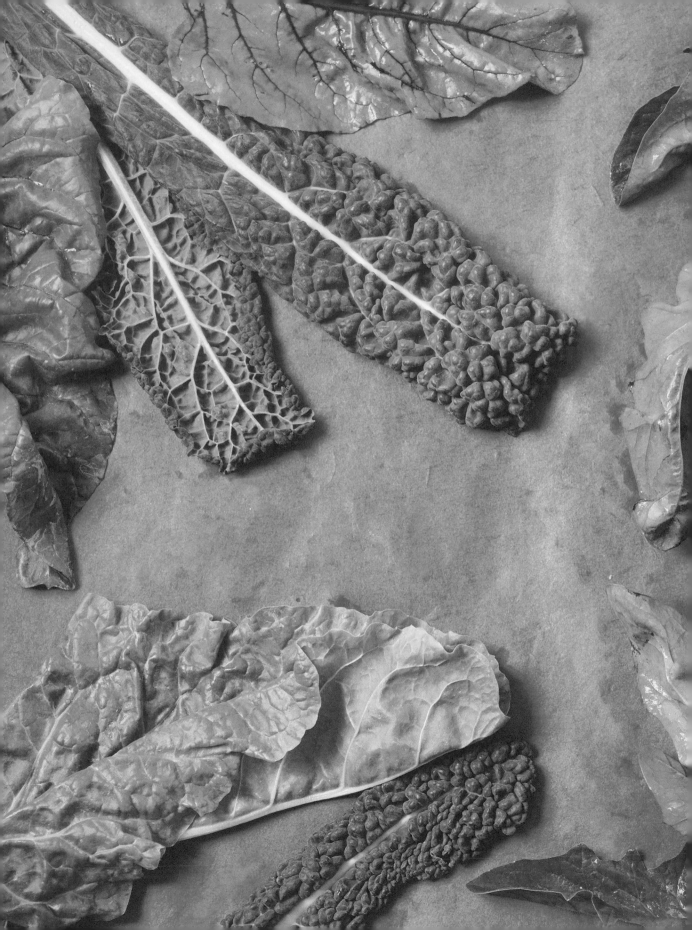

Middle Eastern Lemony Lentil and Almond Salad

Another substantial salad that can be a meal in itself or served as part of a meze of salads. It's important not to overcook the lentils as you want them to hold their shape, so test them after 20 minutes to see how they are doing. Beluga lentils work just as well as the Puy lentils. Pouring on the oil and lemon while the lentils are still warm allows the dressing to penetrate the lentils and the flavours to mingle.

DF GF V

Serves 4–6

225g/8oz of Puy lentils
50g/2oz unblanched almonds,
   whole or roughly chopped
1 tsp ground cumin
3 tbsp olive oil
juice and zest of 2 lemons
250g/9oz cherry tomatoes, halved
100g/3½ oz rocket, baby spinach and
   watercress leaves
2 tbsp chopped coriander
sea salt and freshly ground
   black pepper

Preheat the oven to 200°C/gas 6.

Rinse and drain the lentils, put them in a pan, cover with water and bring to the boil. Skim off any scum that rises to the surface. Turn down the heat, cover and simmer until the lentils are just soft – about 20–25 minutes.

Meanwhile, spread the almonds onto a baking tray and toast in the oven for 10 minutes until crunchy. Once cooked, remove from the tray and leave to cool.

Drain the lentils, put them in a bowl and stir in the cumin, olive oil, lemon juice and zest. Set aside to cool.

Add the tomatoes, rocket, spinach and watercress leaves and almonds to the cooled lentils. Sprinkle on the coriander and season with salt and pepper to taste.

Aubergine, Chickpea and Rocket Salad

Aubergines soak up flavours and oils like sponges. The combination of aubergines, olive oil and tamari creates a delicious soft, oily, saltiness that is hard to resist. The chickpeas provide protein and texture. Adding them to the aubergines while they are still warm means they soak up some of the flavours. You can replace the rocket and coriander with any salad leaves and fresh herbs. Serve warm or at room temperature.

DF   GF   V

Serves 4

4 aubergines
6 tbsp olive oil
2 tbsp tamari soy sauce
2 x 400g/14oz cans chickpeas, drained and rinsed
2 tsp paprika
2 tbsp lemon juice
175g/6oz rocket leaves
4 tbsp chopped coriander
sea salt and freshly ground black pepper

Preheat the oven to 220°C/gas mark 7.

Cut the aubergines in half lengthways, then cut them into 2cm/¾in thick semi-circles. Put them in a baking dish, sprinkle with oil and tamari and mix well. Roast them in the oven for 40–50 minutes until tender, stirring after 20 minutes.

Combine the cooked aubergines with the chickpeas in a large bowl.

Sprinkle on the paprika and lemon juice and season with salt and pepper.

Just before serving, add the rocket and coriander and mix well to distribute the ingredients evenly.

Coleslaw with Toasted Seeds and Lentil Sprouts

This is a tasty and healthy take on a regular coleslaw because instead of high-fat mayonnaise, it uses an oil and vinegar dressing. The addition of sprouted lentils and toasted seeds adds a tasty crunch. It's easy to sprout lentils but it's also possible to buy bags of sprouted beans and lentils. Serve with jacket potatoes or with a range of other salads.

DF GF V

Serves 4

2 tbsp sunflower seeds
2 tbsp pumpkin seeds
¼ of a white cabbage, finely shredded
3 carrots, grated
200g/7oz sprouted lentils or sprouted mung beans
4 tbsp chopped parsley
1 tbsp apple cider vinegar
3 tbsp olive oil
1 tsp toasted sesame oil
sea salt and freshly ground black pepper

Preheat the oven to 200°C/gas mark 6.

Spread the sunflower and pumpkin seeds out on a baking tray and toast in the oven for 10 minutes until just starting to colour.

Combine the cabbage, carrots, toasted seeds, sprouted lentils and parsley in a bowl.

Mix together the cider vinegar, olive oil and toasted sesame oil and pour over the salad. Season with salt and pepper and toss the ingredients together before serving.

Green and White Bean Salad with Avocado Dressing

The clean, fresh look of this salad with its two-tone colour scheme makes you feel healthy just looking at it! The beans can be cooked and combined in advance but the dressing is best made just before eating as avocados oxidise when exposed to air and this can cause discoloration. For a more substantial meal, serve with toasted pitta pockets.

V GF DF

Serves 4 as a starter or side dish

450g/1lb French beans, topped and
  tailed and cut into 2cm/¾in pieces
2 x 400g/14oz cans cannellini
  beans, drained
2 ripe avocados, peeled and stoned
juice of 2 limes
2 tbsp olive oil
4 tbsp chopped parsley
2 little gem lettuces, separated
  into leaves
sea salt and freshly ground
  black pepper

Steam the French beans for about 10 minutes until just tender. Combine them with the cannellini beans in a large bowl.

Put the avocado flesh, lime juice, olive oil, parsley, salt and pepper into a food processor and blitz until you have a smooth texture.

Drizzle the avocado dressing over the beans and stir gently to combine the ingredients.

To serve, spoon the bean mixture onto the little gem leaves.

Warm Butter Bean, Spinach and Sun-dried Tomato Salad

Warming the butter beans allows the flavours of the tamari, lemon and oil to permeate into them. The warm beans also slightly cook the baby spinach. This can be served on its own or with pitta bread and houmous.

DF GF V

Serves 4

2 x 400g/14oz cans butter beans, drained
1 tbsp tamari soy sauce
juice of 1 lemon
225g/8oz baby spinach leaves
3 tbsp roughly chopped sun-dried tomatoes in oil
2 tbsp olive oil
sea salt and freshly ground black pepper

Put the butter beans in a pan with the tamari and lemon juice. Heat gently for a few minutes.

Put the spinach leaves and sun-dried tomatoes in a bowl and spoon the beans over the top.

Drizzle on the olive oil and season with salt and pepper. Stir gently to distribute the ingredients.

Puy Lentils with Roasted Broccoli and Squash

If you haven't tried roasted broccoli now is the time to do so! The florets get slightly charred and crispy while the stem softens in the heat and the oil. Any squash can be used and many do not need to be peeled, making it quicker and easier to prepare. Any whole lentils can be used but dark green Puy lentils go well with the bright orange flesh of the squash. Toasted almonds (see page 24) or feta cheese can be added for a more substantial meal.

DF GF V

Serves 4

125g/4½oz Puy lentils
1 butternut squash, peeled, deseeded and cut into 2cm/¾in chunks
1 large head of broccoli, cut into florets
3 tbsp olive oil
juice of 1 lemon
sea salt and freshly ground black pepper

Preheat the oven to 220°C/gas mark 7.

Put the lentils in a pan, cover with water and bring to the boil. Skim off any scum that rises to the surface, then turn down the heat, cover and simmer for about 25 minutes until the lentils are soft.

Put the butternut squash and broccoli onto separate oven dishes, sprinkle both with olive oil, salt and pepper and give them a stir to coat the vegetables in the oil.

Roast them in the oven for 20 minutes, stir well, then put them back in the oven. They may not need much longer so check after 10 minutes and remove either from the oven when cooked.

Drain the lentils and transfer them to a large bowl. When the vegetables are cooked, mix them in with the lentils.

Sprinkle with lemon juice and season with salt and pepper to taste. Add a drizzle of olive oil if needed.

Quail's Egg and Potato Salad with Vinaigrette Dressing

Of course, it's fine to use hen's eggs for this potato salad but the quail's eggs feel more luxuriant with their higher yolk content. Putting the dressing onto the potatoes while they are hot allows them to soak up the flavour.

DF   GF

Serves 4 as a main meal or 8 as a snack

450g/1lb evenly sized salad potatoes, such as Charlotte, or Pink Fir Apple
12 quail's eggs or 4 hen's eggs, at room temperature
2 tbsp capers
1 tbsp white wine vinegar
1 tbsp French mustard
4 tbsp olive oil
2 tbsp snipped chives
sea salt and freshly ground black pepper

Steam the potatoes whole until soft – about 20 minutes. Check to make sure they are soft by piercing them with a sharp knife.

Half fill another pan with cold water and bring it to the boil. Carefully lower in the quail's eggs and return the water to the boil. Boil the eggs for 2 minutes, drain and refresh in cold water until they have cooled completely. If using hens' eggs, leave them in the boiling water for 6 minutes before removing and cooling.

While the eggs and potatoes are cooking, make the dressing. Mix together the vinegar and mustard in a small jug. Add the olive oil and mix well.

While the potatoes are still hot, cut them into bite-sized pieces and put them into a salad bowl with the capers.

Pour the dressing over the warm potatoes. Season with salt and pepper and leave to cool.

Once the potatoes are cool, shell the eggs and cut them in half. Gently stir the eggs and chives into the potatoes. Add more salt and pepper and a drizzle more oil, if necessary, before serving.

Treats, Cakes & Desserts

Apples and cinnamon, chocolate and nuts, fruit and cream – these are just a few of the classic combinations used to good effect in this collection of delicious, comfort-filled treats. There's something for every occasion, including simple ideas for quick desserts, as well as more lavish recipes for festivals and celebrations. Many of the recipes can be made in advance and stored in a tin or the fridge ready for when needed. And there's no need for anyone to feel deprived as there are even options for those avoiding sugar, wheat, gluten, dairy or eggs.

Magic Chocolate and Cashew Nut Pudding

This is a perennial hit with children and adults alike. One note of warning – when you pour the sauce on before cooking it will look as though you've drowned your cake! Don't be alarmed; the magic part is that during cooking the sauce thickens and sinks while the pudding rises up. Together they create the perfect hot, chocolatey, gooey delight.

V*   GF*

Serves 4–6

For the sponge
50g/2oz cashew nuts
110g/4oz self-raising flour
50g/2oz caster sugar
2 tbsp cocoa powder, sifted
50g/2oz butter or margarine,
  melted, plus extra for greasing
150ml/¼ pint cow's, soya or
  almond milk
a few drops of vanilla extract
icing sugar, sifted, for dusting

For the sauce
110g/4oz light soft brown sugar
2 tbsp cocoa powder, sifted
150ml/¼ pint boiling water

To serve
cream or ice cream

Preheat the oven to 180°C/gas mark 4 and grease a 1 litre/1¾ pint ovenproof dish.

Spread the cashew nuts on the baking tray and bake in the oven for 10 minutes until just starting to colour. Remove, leave to cool, then roughly chop.

To make the sponge, put the flour, sugar, cocoa powder and toasted cashew nuts in a bowl. Add the melted butter, milk and vanilla extract and mix to form a thick batter. Pour into the prepared dish.

To make the sauce, combine the sugar, cocoa powder and boiling water until blended, then pour this over the batter.

Bake in the oven for 35–40 minutes until the top is set but the bottom layer is a gooey sauce.

Sprinkle with a little sifted icing sugar and serve hot with cream or ice cream.

V
---
use margarine and soya or
almond milk, and serve with
a suitable ice cream

GF
---
use gluten-free
self-raising flour

Vegan Blueberry Tart

This tart is a delicious alternative to cheesecake without the dairy, wheat or sugar that most cheesecakes contain. Don't worry, though, the combination of nuts and fruits ensures that it is creamy and delicious. If you do not need it to be gluten free, use ordinary oat flakes rather than the gluten-free ones. You can also add some sugar or honey to the blueberry topping if you want it sweeter.

DF GF V

Serves 6

For the crust
250g/9oz blanched almonds
75g/2½oz pitted dates
50g/2oz gluten-free oat flakes
1 tbsp water
2 tbsp olive oil

For the cashew cream filling
300g/10oz cashew nuts, soaked for 1–2 hours
grated zest and juice of 1 orange
2 tbsp maple syrup
½ tsp vanilla extract or seeds from a vanilla pod
a pinch of salt

For the topping
300g/10oz blueberries
2 tbsp maple syrup (optional)
a little icing sugar, sifted

Preheat the oven to 180°C/gas mark 4 and line a 23cm/9in springform cake tin with baking parchment.

Spread the almonds on a baking tray and bake in the oven for 10 minutes until just starting to colour. Remove and leave to cool, then roughly chop.

To make the crust, blend the toasted almonds, dates, oats, water and oil together in a food processor until they form a thick paste. Add more oats if it feels a bit wet, or add a little water or oil if it feels a bit dry. Press this mixture into the prepared tin and bake in the oven for 15 minutes until just crispy. Leave to cool.

To make the cashew cream, drain and rinse the cashew nuts. Put them in a food processor with the orange zest and juice, maple syrup, vanilla and salt and blend until you have a smooth consistency. Pour two-thirds of this mixture into the cooled pie crust.

To make the topping, put two-thirds of the blueberries, maple syrup, if using, and the remaining cashew cream in the food processor and blend lightly, leaving some texture in the blueberries. Spread this mixture onto the cashew cream and decorate with the remaining blueberries.

Refrigerate for a couple of hours or freeze for an hour before serving sprinkled with icing sugar.

Apple and Blackberry Crumble

The perfect time to make this is late summer or early autumn when apples and blackberries are both in season. Blackberries can be found in abundance along hedgerows in towns, cities and rural areas alike, so be prepared with pots when you go for a walk. If you have lots of blackberries, feel free to increase the quantity. If the blackberry season is over, sultanas, raisins or frozen berries can be used instead.

V*   GF*

Serves 4–6

675g/1½lb cooking apples,
  peeled, cored and chopped
1 tsp cinnamon
110g/4oz blackberries
50g/2oz light soft brown sugar
a little oil, for greasing

For the topping
170g/6oz wholemeal, spelt
  or rice flour or oats
1 tsp cinnamon
85g/3oz butter or margarine, diced
85g/3oz light soft brown sugar
50g/2oz hazelnuts, chopped (optional)

Preheat the oven to 180°C/gas mark 4 and oil a 20cm/8in ovenproof dish.

Put the apples and cinnamon in a pan with a dash of water and simmer until just starting to soften.

Stir in the blackberries and sugar and transfer to the prepared dish.

For the topping, combine the flour or oats and cinnamon in a bowl, then rub in the butter or margarine until you have a breadcrumb-like texture. Add the sugar and hazelnuts, if using, and mix well.

Sprinkle the topping onto the fruit and bake in the oven for 30 minutes until golden on top.

V	GF
use margarine	use gluten-free oats or rice flour

Strawberry Yogurt

This is more delicious than any strawberry yogurt you can buy, as well as being healthier and incredibly easy to make. Raspberries and blueberries make good alternatives to the strawberries. If fresh fruit is not in season, use apple purée or frozen fruit. Serve sprinkled with granola or toasted nuts (see page 24) for a light dessert.

DF* GF SF V*

Serves 4

250g/9oz strawberries, hulled
400g/14oz Greek yogurt

Reserve a few strawberries for decoration and blend the remainder with the yogurt until fairly smooth – it's fine if the strawberries aren't completely blended.

Serve in glasses or bowls and decorate with the reserved whole berries.

DF V

use soya yogurt

Chocolate Orange Mousse

This is a simple but delicious dessert that needs to be made a few hours before eating so that it has time to set in the fridge. As an alternative to the orange juice, add a tablespoon of liqueur, such as Grand Marnier or crème de cassis, or even a shot of cooled espresso for a coffee-flavoured mousse. If you are worried about eating raw eggs, try the Vegan Chocolate Orange Mousse on the next page.

GF

Serves 4

150g/5oz dark chocolate,
  broken into pieces
25g/1oz unsalted butter,
  cut into cubes
3 eggs
2 oranges
2 tbsp caster sugar

Bring a pan of water to the boil, then reduce the heat to a simmer. Place a heatproof bowl over the water, making sure the base is not touching the water, and put the chocolate and butter in the bowl. Stir until they have just melted together and remove from the heat immediately to prevent over-cooking. Set aside to cool slightly.

Meanwhile, separate the eggs and zest and juice the oranges.

Add the sugar to the egg yolks and whisk until you have a thick consistency.

Gently stir the whisked yolks into the melted chocolate and add the orange zest and juice.

Whisk the egg whites until they stand up in soft peaks, then stir a tablespoon of egg white into the chocolate to loosen it. Gently fold the remaining egg whites into the chocolate mixture.

Transfer to small bowls or glasses, cover and refrigerate for at least 2 hours before serving.

Vegan Chocolate Orange Mousse

The tofu in this chocolate mousse is a good vegan substitute for the cream or eggs that are usually found in mousse. Another alternative is to use a couple of ripe avocados. Lemon juice and zest can be used instead of orange juice for a sharper-tasting mousse. Instead of cooking the dates or apricots, you can soak them in orange juice for a few hours to soften.

DF GF SF V

Serves 4

110g/4oz pitted dates or
  dried apricots
grated zest and juice of
  1 large orange
400g/14oz block of silken tofu
4 tbsp cocoa powder
2 tbsp berries or toasted flaked
  almonds (see page 24)
  to decorate (optional)

Put the dates or apricots in a pan with the orange juice and zest and simmer gently for about 15 minutes until soft. Transfer to a bowl and leave to cool.

Once the dates or apricots have cooled, put them in a food processor with the tofu and cocoa powder. Blend until smooth.

Transfer the mixture to small bowls or glasses. Sprinkle with toasted flaked almonds or fresh berries just before serving.

Apricot Tart

This is a fairly easy recipe for a gluten-free fruit tart. It is fine to make it with ordinary pastry but the buckwheat flour and ground almonds give a different flavour and texture from regular pastry. Other fruits that can be used instead of apricots include peaches, nectarines, dessert pears or berries.

DF* GF

Serves 8

150g/5oz buckwheat flour
110g/4oz ground almonds
1 tsp cinnamon
a pinch of salt
110g/4oz butter, diced, or olive oil
about 2–3 tbsp cold water
5 eggs, beaten
1 tbsp cornflour
5 tbsp icing sugar
8–10 apricots, halved and stoned
½ tsp freshly grated nutmeg

Preheat the oven to 180°C/gas mark 4 and oil or line a 23cm/9in flan dish with baking parchment.

Put the buckwheat flour, half the ground almonds, the cinnamon and salt into a bowl. Rub the butter or oil into the flour mixture until you have a breadcrumb-like texture. Add enough cold water to form a firm dough. Cover the bowl and chill in the fridge.

Once chilled, press the dough into the base and sides of the flan case, then prick all over with a fork. This is easier than trying to roll it out. Bake in the oven for 15 minutes until just beginning to crisp up.

Beat the eggs with the cornflour, icing sugar and the rest of the ground almonds.

Arrange the apricots on the cooked flan case. Pour on the egg mixture, grate on the nutmeg and bake for 30 minutes until the egg has set.

DF

use olive oil

Fruit Trifle

Trifle always feels like a real treat but is deceptively easy to make. This recipe is just a matter of piling up the layers. For a super-speedy trifle, buy Madeira cake or trifle sponges and ready-made custard. For a grown-up version, add a dash of sherry or fruit liqueur to the fruit juice. This makes a large trifle to share with family and friends but it is easy to adjust the quantities to suit your needs.

Serves 8

200g/7oz Madeira cake or plain
  sponge cake, sliced
150g/5oz jam
450g/1lb berries, such as strawberries,
  raspberries, blueberries, blackberries
120ml/4fl oz fruit juice
600ml/1 pint custard (ready-made
  or make your own), cooled
600ml/1 pint double cream
flaked almonds, grated chocolate
  or berries, to decorate

Spread the cake slices with the jam, then cut them into squares. Put the cake into a trifle bowl, then scatter the berries on top and pour on the fruit juice.

Spread the custard on top.

Whip the cream until it stands in soft peaks. Dollop this on top of the custard and smooth over.

Cover and refrigerate until needed. Decorate with toasted flaked almonds, grated chocolate or berries just before serving.

Rhubarb Fool

Even people that aren't mad about rhubarb love this creamy dessert. That said, it's also delicious with cooked and puréed apples in place of rhubarb. If you are lucky enough to have a glut of strawberries, they can also be puréed and used instead – leave some whole for decoration and texture. A combination of cream and Greek yogurt can be used to make a lower-fat, but still creamy, dessert.

GF

Serves 4–6

450g/1lb rhubarb, cut into
   2–3cm/¾–1in pieces
50g/2oz light soft brown sugar
50g/2oz butter
300ml/½ pint double cream

Preheat the oven to 180°C/gas mark 4.

Put the rhubarb, sugar and butter in an ovenproof dish and bake in the oven for 15 minutes until the rhubarb has softened.

Once cooked, transfer to a bowl, cool and then chill in the fridge.

Meanwhile, whip the cream until it forms soft peaks but be careful not to over-whip it.

Combine the chilled rhubarb with the whipped cream and serve.

Spiced Bread Pudding

This old-fashioned pudding is a good way to use up stale or leftover bread. The smell of it cooking in the oven will get your taste buds tingling with anticipation.

DF* GF*

Serves 4–6

225g/8oz stale wholemeal bread
110g/4oz mixed currants, sultanas
    and raisins
300ml/½ pint milk plus 4 tbsp
50g/2oz butter or margarine, melted,
    plus extra for greasing
110g/4oz light soft brown sugar
1 tbsp mixed spice
1 egg, beaten
½ tsp freshly grated nutmeg

Break up the bread into pieces and put these in a bowl with the dried fruit. Add the 300ml/½ pint milk and leave to soak for at least 20 minutes.

Preheat the oven to 180°C/gas mark 4 and grease a shallow ovenproof dish.

Stir the melted butter or margarine, sugar and mixed spice into the bread and fruit mixture.

Add the remaining 4 tablespoons of milk to the beaten egg and whisk well before adding it to the bread and fruit. Transfer to the prepared dish and level the surface. Grate the nutmeg over the top.

Bake in the oven for 45–60 minutes until set.

Serve hot or cold.

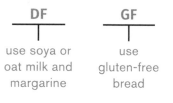

DF	GF
use soya or oat milk and margarine	use gluten-free bread

Fruity Malt Loaf

For many, this recipe will conjure up childhood memories of soft, chewy malt loaf spread with lashings of salted butter eaten after school on winter days. Well, now you can make your own! What's even better about this recipe is that it improves with age so make it a couple of days in advance and store in an airtight container. There is no fat in this loaf – giving the perfect excuse to spread slices liberally with butter before serving!

DF

Serves 8–10

120ml/4fl oz hot black tea
8 tbsp malt extract, plus extra
  for glazing
85g/3oz dark muscovado sugar
200g/7oz mixed raisins and sultanas
a little butter, for greasing
200g/7oz wholemeal flour
1 tsp baking powder
½ tsp bicarbonate of soda
½ tsp mixed spice
2 large eggs, beaten

Combine the hot tea, malt extract, sugar and dried fruit in a mixing bowl and leave to soak while you weigh out the other ingredients, or for longer if you have the time.

Preheat the oven to 170°C/gas mark 3 and grease or line a 900g/2lb loaf tin or two 450g/1lb loaf tins with baking parchment or loaf-tin liners.

Combine the flour, baking powder, bicarbonate of soda and mixed spice in a bowl. Add the beaten eggs to the fruit mixture then stir in the flour mix.

Transfer to the prepared tin and bake for 50 minutes until firm. Remove from the oven and brush with a little warmed malt extract. Leave to cool in the tin for 10 minutes before transferring it onto a cooling rack.

Once cool, wrap in greaseproof paper and store in an airtight container.

Date and Walnut Loaf

This is a coffee-break or tea-time loaf, delicious sliced and spread with butter. The sweetness of the dates means that this recipe contains proportionately less sugar than many other cakes. It is fairly firm, but for a moister loaf add a mashed banana and increase the cooking time by 5–10 minutes.

DF* GF*

Serves 8–10

150g/5oz pitted dates, quartered
grated zest and juice of 1 lemon
85g/3oz walnut pieces
150g/5oz butter, softened, plus
  extra for greasing
150g/5oz light muscovado sugar
3 eggs, beaten
300g/10oz wholemeal
  self-raising flour

Preheat the oven to 200°C/gas mark 6 and line a 900g/2lb loaf tin with baking parchment or a loaf tin liner.

Put the dates and the lemon zest and juice in a bowl.

Spread the walnuts onto a baking tray and toast in the oven for 8 minutes. Remove from the oven and turn the oven temperature down to 170°C/gas mark 3.

Cream together the butter and sugar until fluffy. Stir the eggs into the butter and sugar mixture. Fold in the date and lemon mix. Add 50g/2oz of the walnuts, then fold in the flour.

Spoon the mixture into the prepared tin and arrange the remaining walnuts on top.

Bake for about an hour, or just over, until firm and golden.

GF

use gluten-free self-raising flour

DF

use margarine

Choc Chip Peanut Butter Cookies

These are a quick, easy, gluten-free treat. They also don't contain added sugar other than the small amount in the chocolate chips. For those with allergies to peanuts, other nut or seed butters such as almond, hazelnut or pumpkin seed butter can be used in place of the peanut butter. Honey or maple syrup can be added if a sweeter cookie is desired.

DF*   GF   V*

Makes about 15 cookies

2 ripe bananas
110g/4oz peanut butter
170g/6oz oat flakes, gluten-free
  if wanted
2 tbsp chocolate chips,
  vegan if wanted

DF   V

use vegan
chocolate
chips

Preheat the oven to 180°C/gas mark 4 and line a baking sheet with baking parchment, or use a muffin tin and line with muffin cases.

Mash the bananas in a large bowl.

Add the peanut butter and mix well. Gradually add the oat flakes until you have a thick consistency that holds together. You may need to adjust the amount of oats you use depending on the size and ripeness of the bananas.

Stir in the chocolate chips.

Transfer spoonfuls of the mixture onto the baking sheet or muffin cases and bake for 12–15 minutes until just starting to brown.

No-cook Chocolate Fridge Bars

You don't even need to put the oven on for these healthy snack bars. They are handy to have around as an alternative to commercially available cereal bars, which tend to be full of sugar and processed fats. For this recipe, I've included the quantities in cups so you don't even need to weigh anything – just use a cook's cup measure or an ordinary teacup that holds about 240ml/8fl oz. It is a very forgiving recipe so don't worry if the quantities aren't exact. Feel free to use different nuts and fruits. Alternatives to the dried cherries include goji berries, chopped apricots, chocolate chips, raisins, nuts or seeds.

DF* GF SF V

Makes about 16 bars

130g/4½oz/1 cup blanched almonds
130g/4½oz/1 cup hazelnuts
40g/1½oz/½ cup desiccated coconut
300g/10oz/2 cups medjool dates, pitted
4 tbsp cocoa powder
1 tsp vanilla extract
85g/3oz/6 tbsp softened butter or coconut oil
110g/4oz/1 cup oat flakes or buckwheat flakes
40g/1½oz/⅓ cup dried cherries

Line a 20cm/8in baking tin with baking parchment.

Put the nuts, coconut, dates, cocoa powder, vanilla extract and butter or coconut oil in a food processor and blend until the ingredients hold together. It does not need to be totally smooth.

Transfer to a bowl and stir in the oat flakes or buckwheat flakes and cherries. Mix well.

Press the mixture into the prepared tin, cover and refrigerate for an hour or more before cutting into small bars. Store in an airtight container in the fridge for up to a week.

DF V

use coconut oil

Apricot and Almond Truffles

Fruit and nut truffles are phenomenally quick and easy to make and provide a healthy and delicious treat. Apricots and almonds work well together but there are endless combinations that are also delicious. Try date and walnut, hazelnut and pecan, or cashew and fig. For extra texture, add puffed rice cereal or broken up rice cakes. Grated lemon or orange zest and juice add zinginess. For a Christmas treat, combine cranberries, goji berries, hazelnuts and a dash of rum and serve them in petit four cases.

DF GF SF V

Makes about 15 truffles

130g/4½ oz blanched almonds, lightly toasted (see page 24)
150g/5oz dried apricots
½ tsp almond extract
1–2 tsp honey or maple syrup (optional)
3 tbsp carob powder or cacao powder (optional)
3 tbsp desiccated coconut or sesame seeds

Put the almonds into a food processor and process until they are finely chopped.

Add the apricots, almond extract, honey or maple syrup, and carob or cacao powder if using, and process until you have a thick paste. Add a drop of water, if needed, so that it holds together.

Shape the mixture into walnut-sized balls and roll in the coconut or sesame seeds.

They can be stored in an airtight container in the fridge for up to a week.

Apple, Cinnamon and Pecan Cake

Oil is used in this recipe as an alternative to butter or margarine. It is a moist cake perfect for autumn when apples are in abundance. Bramley's work well, but other apples can also be used. The pecans can be replaced with other nuts, and raisins or sultanas can be added.

DF GF*

Serves 6–8

a little butter or oil, for greasing
225g/8oz wholemeal self-raising flour
¼ tsp salt
1 tsp cinnamon
1 tsp mixed spice
350g/12oz cooking apples, peeled, cored and chopped
110g/4oz light soft brown sugar
1 egg, beaten
110g/4oz pecan nuts, toasted (see page 117)
4 tbsp olive oil
150ml/¼ pint oat or soya milk

Preheat the oven to 190°C/gas mark 5 and grease or line a 19cm/7½in square cake tin with baking parchment.

Combine the flour, salt, cinnamon and mixed spice in a bowl. Add the apples, sugar, egg, most of the nuts and the oil to the dry ingredients and stir well. Add enough milk to help the mixture hold together.

Spread the mixture into the prepared tin and sprinkle with the remaining nuts. Bake in the oven for about 30–35 minutes until it is firm to touch.

Leave to cool in the tin, then cut into squares to serve.

GF
|
use gluten-free
self-raising flour

Apricot and Almond Cake

Appearances can be deceptive! This cake doesn't look that fancy but it tastes absolutely delicious. The apricots and almonds work perfectly together to provide crunch, sweetness and moisture. There is very little sugar in the recipe compared to many other cakes because the apricots provide ample fruity sweetness.

EF GF* V*

Serves 8

180g/6oz dried apricots, chopped
250ml/9fl oz soya milk
1 tsp almond extract
110g/4oz blanched almonds
110g/4oz wholemeal flour
110g/4oz ground almonds
1½ tbsp baking powder
110g/4oz butter or margarine
50g/2oz light soft brown sugar

GF

use rice or buckwheat flour

DF V

use margarine

Soak the apricots in the soya milk and almond extract for a few hours.

Preheat the oven to 220°C/gas mark 7 and grease a 20cm/8in cake tin.

Spread the almonds onto a baking tray and roast in the oven for 10 minutes until they start to brown.

Turn the oven temperature down to 170°C/gas mark 3. Reserve 8 almonds for decoration, then roughly chop the remainder.

Put the flour, ground almonds and baking powder in a bowl and mix together.

Melt the butter or margarine and sugar in a small pan over a low heat, then add it to the flour mixture and mix well. Stir in the chopped almonds and the apricot and soya milk mixture.

Transfer to the prepared cake tin, decorate with the reserved whole almonds and bake for 50 minutes, or until firm to touch and a knife comes out cleanly.

Allow to cool before removing from the tin.

Strawberry Ripple Ice Cream

It is not essential to freeze the fruit in advance but the ice cream will set more quickly if you do. Any soft fruit can be used in place of the strawberries. For a raspberry ripple ice cream, rub the raspberries through a sieve after puréeing to remove the seeds. Otherwise try peaches, apricots, blackcurrants or mangos. This ice cream can be made without the yogurt if you want a purely fruit-based dessert.

GF EF

Serves 4

150g/5oz strawberries, frozen
2 ripe bananas, peeled, cut into chunks and frozen
2 tbsp icing sugar (optional)
250g/9oz coconut flavoured Greek yogurt

Purée the frozen strawberries and bananas in a food processor along with the icing sugar, if using.

Put the yogurt in a container with a lid and swirl in the fruit purée. Put the lid on and freeze for 30 minutes or more until just set. If you freeze it for longer, remove from the freezer 15 minutes before serving.

Fruity Lollies

These ice lollies are quick to make and can be made in advance ready for when a cooling treat is needed. Although ice lollies feel like an indulgence, these can be eaten guilt free as they are made entirely from fruit. The bananas provide a creamy base that can be combined with a range of soft fruits. Any fruit juice can be used or try diluted fruit cordial instead.

DF GF SF V

Makes 4 lollies

1 large mango, peeled and
   stone removed
2 ripe bananas, peeled
240ml/8fl oz orange juice
a few raspberries, crumbled
a few blueberries
a few small strawberries, halved

Place the mango flesh, bananas and orange juice in a food processor or blender and blend until smooth.

Pour a quarter of the mixture into ice-lolly moulds, then add a few raspberries, another quarter of the mixture and the blueberries, another quarter of the mixture and the strawberries, then the remaining mixture. Insert lolly sticks and freeze until solid.

Luxury Chocolate Cake

There are many recipes for chocolate cake and, let's face it, if you throw together chocolate, sugar, butter and eggs you can't go far wrong! However, this cake is a bit special as it is made with ground almonds instead of flour. If the cooking time is reduced, the result has the gooey texture of chocolate brownies. For a coffee-flavoured chocolate cake, add a couple of tablespoons of cooled strong, black coffee to the chocolate while it's melting.

GF

Serves 10

300g/10oz cooking chocolate
  or very dark chocolate
150g/5oz unsalted butter
250g/9oz golden caster sugar
5 large eggs
110g/4oz ground almonds
a pinch of salt
cocoa or icing sugar, sifted,
  for dusting

To serve
a large handful of raspberries
whipped cream, crème fraîche
  or Greek yogurt

Preheat the oven to 180°C/gas mark 4 and line a 23cm/9in cake tin with baking parchment.

Fill a pan half full of water and put on to the boil. Sit a bowl above the water and not touching it, and put the chocolate, butter and caster sugar into the bowl.

Stir the chocolate, butter and sugar until they melt and are well mixed. Remove from the heat.

Whisk together the eggs, ground almonds and salt, then add them to the chocolate mixture.

Transfer to the prepared tin, smooth the top and bake in the oven for 35 minutes until just set.

Leave to cool, then top with raspberries and dust with cocoa, or icing sugar if you prefer. Serve with whipped cream, crème fraîche or Greek yogurt.

Conversion Table

Weights		Length		Volume		
metric	imperial	metric	imperial	ml	fl oz	pints
7.5g	¼oz	5mm	¼in	5ml	1 tsp	
15g	½oz	1cm	½in	15ml	1 tbsp	
20g	¾oz	2cm	¾in	30ml	1fl oz	
30g	1oz	2.5cm	1in	40ml	1½fl oz	
40g	1½oz	4cm	1½in	55ml	2fl oz	
50g	2oz	6cm	2in	70ml	2½fl oz	
65g	2¼oz	7cm	2½in	85ml	3fl oz	
75g	2½oz	7.5cm	3in	100ml	3½fl oz	
80g	2¾oz	10cm	4in	120ml	4fl oz	
85g	3oz	18cm	7in	130ml	4½fl oz	
100g	3½oz	19cm	7½in	150ml	5fl oz	¼ pint
110g	4oz	20cm	8in	170ml	5½fl oz	
125g	4½oz	22cm	8½in	185ml	6½fl oz	
150g	5oz	23cm	9in	200ml	7fl oz	
170g	6oz	25cm	10in	240ml	8fl oz	
180g	6½oz	27cm	11in	250ml	9fl oz	
200g	7oz	30cm	12in	270ml	9½fl oz	
225g	8oz	35cm	14in	300ml	10fl oz	½ pint
240g	8½oz	38cm	15in	350ml	12fl oz	
250g	9oz			400ml	14fl oz	
300g	10oz			425ml	15fl oz	
310g	11oz			450ml	16fl oz	¾ pint
340g	12oz			465ml	16½fl oz	
370g	13oz			600ml	20fl oz	1 pint
400g	14oz			700ml	25fl oz	
425g	15oz			750ml	26fl oz	1¼ pints
450g	1lb			900ml	30fl oz	1½ pints
500g	1lb 2oz			1 litre	35fl oz	1¾ pints
565g	1¼lb			1.5 litres	53fl oz	2 pints
600g	1lb 5oz					
680g	1½lb					
700g	1lb 9oz					
750g	1lb 10oz					
800g	1¾lb					
900g	2lb					
1kg	2lb 3oz					
1.1kg	2lb 7oz					
1.4kg	3lb					
1.5kg	3½lb					
1.8kg	4lb					
2kg	4½lb					
2.3kg	5lb					
2.7kg	6lb					
3.1kg	7lb					
3.6kg	8lb					
4.5kg	10lb					

Oven temperatures

temperature	fan	conventional	gas
Very cool	100°C	110°C/225°F	gas mark ¼
Very cool	120°C	130°C/250°F	gas mark ½
Cool	130°C	140°C/275°F	gas mark 1
Slow	140°C	150°C/300°F	gas mark 2
Moderately slow	160°C	170°C/325°F	gas mark 3
Moderate	170°C	180°C/350°F	gas mark 4
Moderately hot	180°C	190°C/375°F	gas mark 5
Hot	190°C	200°C/400°F	gas mark 6
Very hot	200°C	220°C/425°F	gas mark 7
Very hot	220°C	230°C/450°F	gas mark 8
Hottest	230°C	240°C/475°F	gas mark 9

Notes

Notes on the Recipes
Unless otherwise stated:
Use medium fruit and vegetables.
Use fresh ingredients, including herbs and spices.
Do not mix metric and imperial measurements.
All spoon measurements are level.
1 tsp = 5ml   1 tbsp = 15ml.
Oven temperatures are for conventional ovens; reduce by 10°C for fan ovens.
The serving suggestions are not included in the dietary symbols at the top of the recipes, so remember to choose appropriate ingredients.

Reasonable care has been taken to ensure the accuracy of the recipes and instructions in this book. However, any liability for inaccuracies or errors relating to the material contained within the book is expressly excluded to the fullest extent permitted by law. You may not always achieve the desired results.

Oven temperatures vary between different appliances and different equipment may affect the desired outcome. Neither the National Trust, National Trust (Enterprises) Ltd nor Pavilion Books Ltd accept any responsibility or liability for the end results of the recipes featured in this book.

Warning: recipes containing raw eggs are unsuitable for pregnant women or young children.

Index

Acknowledgements

Huge thanks to all residents and visitors of Lower Shaw Farm, in particular to Matt and Andrea, for allowing me to cook and experiment in the farmhouse kitchen for 17 happy years. It has been a huge learning experience and this book would not have been possible without your faith in me. Also big thanks to all friends and family who have endured the eccentricities of my cooking experiments over the years. And much gratitude to Katie at the National Trust and Lucy at Pavillion Books for your positivity throughout the process of bringing the book to fruition.

First published in the United Kingdom in 2016 by National Trust Books
1 Gower Street
London WC1E 6HD

An imprint of Pavilion Books Group

ISBN 9781909881839

A CIP catalogue record for this book is available from the British Library.

10 9 8 7 6 5 4 3 2 1

Reproduction by Mission Productions, Hong Kong
Printed by Toppan Leefung Printing Ltd, China

Home Economist: Sara Lewis
Food Photographer: William Shaw
Prop Stylist: Alexander Breeze
Senior Commissioning Editor: Peter Taylor
Senior Editor: Lucy Smith
Copy Editor: Wendy Hobson
Designer: Lee-May Lim

This book can be ordered direct from the publisher at the website: www.pavilionbooks.com, or try your local bookshop. Also available at National Trust shops or www.shop.nationaltrust.org.uk.